The HERITAGE TREES

of BRITAIN & NORTHERN IRELAND

The HERITAGE TREES

of BRITAIN & NORTHERN IRELAND

Jon Stokes *and* Donald Rodger
Photographs by Archie Miles *and* Edward Parker

Foreword by Thomas Pakenham

Published in association with the Tree Council

CONSTABLE • LONDON

Constable & Robinson Ltd
3 The Lanchesters
162 Fulham Palace Road
London W6 9ER
www.constablerobinson.com

First published in the UK in 2004 by Constable,
an imprint of Constable & Robinson Ltd

A copy of the British Library Cataloguing in
Publication data is available from the British Library

ISBN 1-84119-959-1

Printed and bound in Italy
The paper used in this book is acid free and from sustainable sources

Book design by Carter Graphics, Worcester
Art direction by Archie Miles

Opposite title page: Detail of one of the fraternal Four, Borrowdale (see page 78).
Page 8: Ancient oak in Windsor Great Park.
Page 11: The Crowhurst Yew from the other side (see page 118).

Contents

continued overleaf…

ENGLAND (continued)

WALES

Kirkwall

Thurso

① ② ③
Inverness

Aberdeen

Mallaig

SCOTLAND

④ ⑤ ⑥ ⑧ ⑩
⑦ ⑨
Oban ⑪
Perth Dundee

⑫ ⑬
⑭ ⑮
⑱ ⑯ ⑰ Edinburgh
Glasgow ㉒ ㉔
㉕ ㉓
⑳ ㉑ ⑲
㉗
Ayr ㉖
NORTHERN ㉘ ㉚
IRELAND ㉙
Londonderry Dumfries
Carlisle Newcastle
㉛ Belfast
㉜ Armagh Middlesbrough
㉝
㉞

IRELAND Dublin ㉟ ㊱
㊲
Leeds
Kingston-upon-Hull

Manchester ENGLAND
Liverpool Sheffield
⑧① ⑧⓪ ⑦⑨ ㊵
Wrexham ⑦⑧ ㊳ Derby ㊴
WALES ⑦⑦ ㊶ ㊷
Birmingham Norwich
⑧② ⑦⑥ ㊺ ㊹ ㊻
⑦⑤ ⑦④ ㊸ Cambridge
Aberystwyth Northampton ㊼
⑧③ ⑦① ⑦② Ipswich
⑦③
⑧④ Gloucester Oxford Colchester
⑧⑥ Swansea ⑧⑦ ⑧⑧ London ㊾
⑧⑤ ⑦⓪ ⑥⑨ ⑥⓪ ㊿ ⑤① ㊽
Cardiff ⑥⑧ ⑤⑨ ⑤⓪ ⑤②
Bristol ⑤⑧ ⑤④ ⑤③
⑥⑥ ⑥⑦ ⑥① Salisbury ⑤⑦ ⑤⑥ ⑤⑤ Dover
Southampton Brighton
Exeter ⑥③ ⑥②
⑥⑤ ⑥④
Plymouth

Penzance

0   20   40   60 miles

0 20 40 60 80 100 km

Foreword

Why do we feel for trees? This was the question which Alexander von Humboldt, the great German naturalist, tried to answer 200 years ago. 'We feel for them', he said, 'because we identify with them. Like us, they are small and helpless when they are young. Like us, they take pride in their power when they come to maturity. And like us, they come to a tottering old age when they are once again dependent on others for survival'.

It's the third stage, I think, that evokes – or should evoke – our strongest sympathy. Look at the great oak on the village green that has seen 10 generations of men and women complete their life spans around it. It was the clock, as Tennyson puts it, that 'beats out the little lives of men'. Once it was all-encompassing: the great mother tree of the district, like the Royal Oak, the Boscobel tree that gave shelter to King Charles II when he was on the run from his enemies. Now, after 500 years or more, the great clock is running down. Most of the massive limbs that once threatened the church roof have decayed and fallen. At its heart is a hollow the size of a cave. Now its life is full of indignities – and dangers. Rubbish accumulates inside the cave. Children torment it with fires. Every storm brings down more branches. But this is more than a historical monument. It's a living museum. What could be more worth taking trouble to save?

Perhaps museum is too dusty a word. Museums can be unspiritual places. For many of us, to stand under a great tree (or hug it, and why not?) is an intensely spiritual experience. Try going to Windsor Great Park one afternoon in spring. Close to the main road that connects the two motorways to north and south, are lines of ancient oak trees – 'dodders' as they were once called. Enthusiasts claim that there are more ancient trees in this one park than in the whole of France or Germany. Perhaps this is an exaggeration. But the sight is stunning, a scene from Tolkien: thousands of ancient trees marching like an army – some limping, some stricken, others still huge despite every infirmity. The marvellous thing is that these relics of Tudor and Plantagenet forests are safe. The Crown authorities that manage Windsor Park are proud of this extraordinary heritage and pay to keep it secure. If only this were true of other ancient trees in Britain. Tree preservation orders, cheerfully imposed by local authorities, give them some degree of protection. But these legal orders are easily sidestepped – especially if a tree is old and would cost money to feed and to care for.

Old trees, like old people, can be inspiring. Their fortitude and stoicism is good to experience. And, if we do the talking, they make excellent listeners. Life burns bright in them, whatever their handicaps. Go and look at an ancient oak in May, just when the buds begin to break. The many-lobed oak leaves are as bright and fresh as any young sapling's. And by October you can collect the acorns, crunching under foot like pebbles, to grow a new oak forest that will last another 1000 years.

Thomas Pakenham, June 2004.

Introduction

Every community has its special trees. Some are widely appreciated and much visited, others are local landmarks, known only to a few people, but all are worthy of celebration. We have set out to do just that with this book by highlighting some of the outstanding heritage trees of Britain and Northern Ireland – the significant, the celebrated and the curious. They are all trees with a story and every one of them can be visited by the public, even those in private gardens.

From the oldest, rarest or largest to some of the most historically or culturally famous, the examples in this book underline the fundamental importance of such trees to the heritage of England, Wales, Scotland and Northern Ireland. Some are as important as stately homes and castles yet, unlike buildings, there is no specific protection for trees of historic significance. The stories told here are by no means the only ones worth reading. There are many more, far more than can be done justice in one volume. However, some of these witnesses to history will be lost because there is inadequate recognition of their value. Any legal shield that exists is coincidental, not by design. We are fortunate that many are still standing.

The Tree Council, which is made up of the organisations concerned with tree planting, care and conservation nationally, is therefore advocating a system that will specifically safeguard heritage trees for future generations. We can enjoy these special trees today largely thanks to the individuals, past and present, who have cared for them and ensured their survival. However, whilst some trees may remain in benevolent ownership, it is not enough to assume that this will always be so. It takes only one person in the life of a tree to mutilate or destroy it. We want protective provision that will encourage the custodians of heritage trees to look after them, and provide support and advice on their care. As the UK's lead tree campaigning partnership, we are working to promote this concept of protected status for 'green monuments'.

The principle is not as extraordinary as it may seem. The value of important trees is already recognised in other countries. In some places, trees above a certain size have automatic protection, whilst in others it extends to any tree over a certain age. This protection is known by various names, but it all comes back to the undisputed historical, cultural and ecological value of these most amazing living things. This book of stories, and the stunning portraits of their subjects, brings home the importance of protecting our tree heritage.

The Castle Leod Redwood

In the grounds of Castle Leod, off the A834 half a mile (0.8 kilometres) east of Strathpeffer, Easter Ross, Highland. The grounds are open to the public at certain times throughout the year.

The tallest giant redwood *(Sequoiadendron giganteum)* so far recorded in the United Kingdom stands in the grounds of Castle Leod, Strathpeffer. It measures a staggering 170 feet (52 metres) tall and its equally impressive trunk has a girth of 29 feet 3 inches (8.9 metres). The tree is also notable as one of the few surviving original introductions of this species, brought to these shores by the Scottish botanist and plant collector John Matthew in 1853.

The estate records it as being planted in 1853 to commemorate the first birthday of Francis Mackenzie, Viscount Tarbat and later Earl of Cromartie. Regular measurements taken since 1891 show rapid growth. By 1954, only 100 years after planting, the tree had already topped 98 feet (30 metres) and the beautifully flared trunk had attained a girth of 22 feet 9 inches (6.9 metres). The tree is a handsome and stately specimen, with a shapely, spire-like crown so typical of the species.

The giant redwood is often referred to as 'Wellingtonia', a name given to it by John Lindley of the Horticultural Society. He thought it appropriate that the world's most impressive tree should commemorate the Duke of Wellington, who had died the year before (see page 126).

The champion giant redwood may be seen to the immediate right of the castle.

1550
Sweet Chestnut

The tree with the oldest recorded planting date in the Scotland is the superb sweet chestnut *(Castanea sativa)* at Castle Leod, Strathpeffer. Estate records show the tree was planted in 1550 by John Mackenzie (1480 – 1556), 9th Chief of Kintail and a Privy Councillor to King James V and Mary, Queen of Scots.

The tree is an outstanding specimen of very large size. The long, clean trunk measures 26 feet 7 inches (8.1 metres) in girth and the lofty canopy has attained a height of 92 feet (28 metres). Historical measurements of the trunk's girth suggest a relatively slow rate of growth. In 1867 the girth was 18 feet 2 inches (5.5 metres), in 1908 21 feet 6 inches (6.4 metres), and in 1938 23 feet 3 inches (7.1 metres). The thick, fissured bark on the bole displays a strong spiral twist that is very characteristic of old sweet chestnuts. The angle of the spiral tends to increase as trees age, although the grain of the underlying timber normally remains vertical. Despite its very great age, the Castle Leod tree is in remarkably good health. Unfortunately, a second, smaller sweet chestnut also dating from 1550 was lost in a gale in 1979.

In the grounds of Castle Leod, off the A834 road about half a mile (0.8 kilometres) east of Strathpeffer, Easter Ross, Highland. The grounds are open to the public at certain times throughout the year.

The Kilravock Castle Layering Beech

Beeches *(Fagus sylvatica)* with a tendency to layer are extremely rare in Scotland. Of the very few specimens known to exist, the finest and largest is that which graces the grounds of Kilravock Castle, Inverness-shire. The huge trunk measures 16 feet (4.9 metres) in girth at 3.3 feet (1 metre) from ground level, and it is surrounded by low, snaking limbs which bend to the ground and take root. Some of the layered stems are of considerable size and now form small trees in their own right. The tree has been repeatedly pollarded in the past and the typically dense, multi-stemmed crown is still in good condition. Thought to have been planted in the latter half of the seventeenth century, it is of considerable age for a species not known for longevity.

The tree is also known as the 'Kissing Beech', after a member of an early (or a previous) owner's family and a housemaid were witnessed in an illicit embrace under its spreading limbs. The extensive carving of lovers' names on the bark suggests that many others have used this tree as a rendezvous. The attraction of lovers to beech trees has led to many other old beeches being known as "Trysting Trees", because "of their smooth grey bark in which letters of devotion, hearts and arrows of desire have long been scribed." [1]

Kilravock Castle (pronounced Kilrawck), built in 1460, has seen many famous visitors over the centuries, including Mary, Queen of Scots in 1562 and Robert Burns in 1787. Bonnie Prince Charlie is reputed to have been entertained within its thick walls the day before the Battle of Culloden in 1746.

On a low bank alongside the driveway to Kilravock Castle, on the B9091 road between Croy and Clephanton, approximately 10 miles (16 kilometres) east of Inverness and the A9. The castle is administered by Ellel Ministries as a hotel and religious retreat. Access is available only with permission.

Rannoch Rowan

An expansive view across Rannoch Moor shows the true isolation of this tree.

Probably the loneliest tree in Britain is the rowan *(Sorbus aucuparia)* that stands in splendid isolation in the desolate wilderness of Rannoch Moor. It perches on top of a giant boulder, its windswept crown bearing testament to the extreme exposure with which it has to contend. Remarkably, the tree has managed to maintain a hold in the crevices of its lichen-encrusted pedestal, its roots somehow seeking sustenance from a deep fissure in the rock. This lonely rowan is now a well-known landmark on the busy A82 road.

The secret of the tree's survival is its elevated position, which keeps it out of reach of the relentless grazing by sheep and deer. Rowan, a species native to Scotland, is an opportunist of the tree world, and this particular tree has carved out its own niche in a harsh environment.

Rannoch Moor was not always so bleak and treeless. Between 5000 and 2500 years ago, Scotland's climate was drier and more continental, causing the bogs to dry out briefly. A vast forest of birch and pine colonised the moor, only to disappear as the climate gradually changed again. All that now remains are countless stumps entombed in a peaty grave, and a small remnant of native pinewood known as the Black Wood of Rannoch.

Beside the A82 trunk road between Glen Coe and Bridge of Orchy. Public access is available.

In a private field near Slatich Farm, about 10 miles (16 kilometres) along Glen Lyon from Fortingall, near Aberfeldy. The tree stands close to the public road, from where it can easily be viewed.

The
Glen Lyon
Ash

One of the largest and oldest examples of native ash *(Fraxinus excelsior)* resides in Perthshire's beautiful Glen Lyon. The moss–covered trunk has an exceptional girth measuring 21 feet (6.4 metres), the largest so far recorded for this species in Scotland. Once reaching 98 feet (30 metres) in height, the crown has been heavily cut back to a stump of some 13 feet (4 metres).

The tree appears to have been pollarded at various times throughout its life. This ancient form of tree management involves cutting the top off the tree to stimulate the production of numerous straight shoots. These are harvested periodically to provide a sustainable source of timber and animal fodder. Pollarding is normally carried out between 6 feet 6 inches and 13 feet (2 to 4 metres) above ground level so that the young growth is out of the reach of grazing animals. While pollarding may look rather severe when newly carried out, it can be an effective method for securing the future of veteran trees. The Glen Lyon ash has certainly benefited, and is putting on vigorous new growth.

It is possible that this veteran may be around 300 to 400 years old. This is exceptional for ash, which is not known as a long-lived species. Under normal circumstances in Scotland, ash can be expected to attain a maximum age of 200 to 250 years before decay and decline set in.

The churchyard at Fortingall, about 8 miles (13 kilometres) west of Aberfeldy, Perthshire. Free public access is available all year.

The Fortingall Yew

Estimated to be perhaps 5,000 years old, the Fortingall Yew *(Taxus baccata)* stands at the geographical heart of Scotland. It is believed to be the most ancient tree in the United Kingdom, and is probably even the oldest living thing in Europe.

The tree was first described in 1769 by the Hon. Daines Barrington [1], who measured its circumference at 52 feet (16 metres). By July 1833 [2] Dr Neil found that large amounts had been cut away "by the country people, with the view of forming quechs or drinking cups, and other relics, which visitors were in the habit of purchasing". The trunk then resembled a semicircular wall, although new spray and a few young branches were growing to a height of up to 30 feet (9 metres).

In 1854, Loudon [3] said "its age is unknown, but it has long been a mere shell, forming an arch through which funeral processions were accustomed to pass".

Today this venerable tree is still a very impressive sight and is enclosed by a wall built to create a sanctuary for its undisturbed growth. Its trunk now comprises several separate elements and without knowing the tree's long history it would be difficult to regard it as a single tree.

Wood engraving of the tree from *Sylva Britannica* by J.G. Strutt (1830).

The Birnam Oak

William Shakespeare
(1564 – 1616)

An ancient sessile oak *(Quercus petraea)* standing on the banks of the River Tay near the village of Birnam is said to be the last survivor of the legendary Birnam Wood, immortalised in Shakespeare's *Macbeth*:

> *"Macbeth shall never vanquish'd be until*
> *Great Birnam Wood to high Dunsinane Hill*
> *Shall come against him."*

The witches' prophecy literally came true, when Malcolm's army camouflaged itself with branches from the great wood and took by surprise Macbeth's stronghold at Dunsinane, 12 miles (20 kilometres) to the south east:

> *"As I did stand my watch upon the hill,*
> *I looked toward Birnam and anon methought*
> *The wood began to move."*

The tragic Macbeth then meets his gruesome end.

On the south bank of the River Tay at Birnam, Perthshire, accessible via a sign-posted footpath from Dunkeld bridge and another from the Birnam House Hotel in the centre of the village. Free public access is available throughout the year.

It is unlikely that this fine old veteran, sometimes known as 'Macbeth's Oak', was around to furnish Malcolm's soldiers with greenery when the battle was reputedly fought, in 1057. It is, however, several centuries old and represents a living relic of the great medieval oakwood that once clothed the banks of the Tay.

The trunk boasts an impressive girth of 18 feet (5.5 metres) and a widely spreading canopy composed of long, horizontal limbs. A stately survivor of a bygone age, its literary connection has resulted in its becoming one of Scotland's better-known heritage trees.

The Parent Larch

DUNKELD LARCHES

The Dunkeld Larches
by G W Wilson,
from *The Larch*
by C Y Michie (1882).

With a girth of 18 feet 6 inches (5.6 metres), this is one of the largest European larches *(Larix decidua)* in the United Kingdom. It was planted after a visit to Dunkeld by a "Mr Menzies of Megeny in Glenlyon, who in 1738 brought a few small larch plants in his portmanteau, five of which he left for Duke James of Atholl."[1] Of those five, one was cut by the gardener about 1790 "by mistake",[1] and two were felled in 1809. The present tree is the last of the original five planted by Duke James. His successors, notably the 4th Duke (John, 1755 - 1830), known as the Planting Duke, were increasingly absorbed with planting European larch on the hills of Atholl. By 1830 the total planted by all the Dukes exceeded 14 million larch trees covering nearly 10,500 acres (4,250 hectares).[1]

This tree and its now dead companions had already been dubbed the "Parent Larches" by 1812 [2] because they provided some of the seed for the early plantings. The remaining tree now stands as a monument to the tree-planting feats achieved by the Dukes and, although an old tree, it is still a magnificent specimen.

Alongside the footpath that runs west of the main (north) car park in Dunkeld and skirts the edge of Dunkeld Cathedral, where the path meets the woodland on the edge of the grounds of the Hilton Dunkeld House Hotel, 15 miles (24 kilometres) north of Perth. Free public access is available.

The Meikleour Beech Hedge

Since 1966, the impressive beech *(Fagus sylvatica)* hedge that runs adjacent to the busy A93 road has been officially recognised as the tallest in the world. This over-powering 'green wall' stands 120 feet (36.6 metres) tall at its northern end and gradually diminishes to a mere 80 feet (24.4 metres) at its southern extremity, with an average height of 100 feet (30 metres). About 1738 feet (530 metres) long, it is cut and re-measured every 10 years, a complex operation that takes four men about six weeks to complete.

An Edwardian postcard of the hedge.

The hedge is believed to have been laid out and planted in the autumn of 1745, the year of the second Jacobite uprising, by Jean Mercer and her husband, Robert Murray Nairne. Following the death of her husband at the battle of Culloden a year later, Jean Mercer moved to Edinburgh to live with friends, leaving the young hedge to grow untended. A more romantic version of events has it that the gardeners who planted the hedge took up arms for Bonnie Prince Charlie and perished on the field of Culloden. Their hedge was left to grow untended towards the heavens as a living monument to their memory. Whatever the explanation for its great height, the hedge is now a world-beating wonder and a popular attraction for tourists.

Alongside the A93 trunk road about 4 miles (6.4 kilometres) south of Blairgowrie, Perthshire. Parking and an interpretation board are available.

The Camperdown Elm

The Camperdown elm *(Ulmus glabra* 'Camperdownii'*)* is a natural mutant of Scotland's native wych elm. It was discovered by chance about 1835 growing wild in woodland by the Earl of Camperdown's head forester, David Taylor. Intrigued by its alien appearance, Taylor carefully lifted and transplanted the tree to the landscaped grounds that surround Camperdown House, on the outskirts of Dundee. Before long, interest in this outlandish variety grew and the Camperdown elm provided the early cuttings from which it was to be widely propagated. The instantly recognisable form of the tree soon became a common sight in parks, gardens and cemeteries.

The original tree survives to this day, and has so far escaped the ravages of Dutch elm disease. Standing no more than 10 feet (3 metres) tall, the weeping branches extend to the ground. However, it is the bizarre branch architecture that is its most remarkable feature. The crown consists of a mass of heavily convoluted and twisted branches knotted together in dense clusters. These painfully and impossibly double back repeatedly on one another to create a marvellous living sculpture unrivalled by any other variety of tree.

Camperdown Park, on the north western outskirts of Dundee, is owned and managed by Dundee City Council and free public access is available at all times.

This magnificent tree was grown from seed brought back from the Pacific north west of North America by celebrated Scottish botanist and explorer David Douglas – hence its name. Most likely the seed was collected in 1825 from the lower reaches of the Columbia River, near Fort Vancouver, arriving in Britain in 1827. The seeds were sown, the seedlings raised in a nursery and then planted out at Scone in 1834, the year that Douglas was killed on the slopes of Mauna Kea, Hawaii, when he fell into a wild cattle trap. He is buried at Kawaiahoa Church, Honolulu. Elwes [1] said that, "the tree was transplanted to its current position in 1850."

Douglas was born within the grounds of Scone Palace and worked there as a gardener. In 1820 he was accepted for a post at the Botanic Gardens, Glasgow, under Dr William Hooker, and he began his plant-hunting expeditions in 1823. Among his other discoveries are the noble and grand firs and the Sitka spruce, now widely recognised as one of the United Kingdom's most important timber trees.

Grown from the first seed to arrive in Britain and planted close to his birthplace, this Douglas fir *(Pseudotsuga menziesii)* is a living memorial to a great plant hunter whose discoveries shaped much of the commercial forest landscape of Britain.

> *Next to the ruins of the old village of Scone, in the grounds of Scone Palace, a short distance north of Perth on the A93 road to Braemar. The house and grounds are normally open from Good Friday to mid-October and admission charges apply. Tours are available in winter by prior appointment with the estate office.*

The Scone Douglas Fir

The Wishing Tree

This lone, wind-blasted hawthorn (*Crataegus monogyna*) growing in the wilds of Argyll is one of the few known 'wishing trees' in Scotland. It is encrusted with coins that have been pressed into the thin bark by generations of superstitious travellers over the centuries, each coin representing a wish. Every available space on the main trunk bristles with money, even the smaller branches and exposed roots. This magical tree provides a living connection with the ancient folklore and customs of Scotland.

Hawthorn as a species is deeply enshrined in the tradition and mythology of the British Isles. In pagan times it was regarded as the prime symbol of fertility and was celebrated as a powerful harbinger of spring. It has long been associated with the ancient rites of Mayday, the blossoms of 'the May' symbolising love and betrothal. It was also thought to possess strong healing and magical qualities.

Why a nondescript hawthorn in the Argyll wilderness has assumed such superstitious significance is lost in the mists of time. It has undoubtedly been revered as a special tree for many years, as its substantial hoard of cash will testify. Unfortunately, the tree has succumbed to its harsh environment and is now lying in its enclosure.

By a rough moorland track about 2 miles (3.2 kilometres) south of Ardmaddy House, near the bridge over the Atlantic to the Isle of Seil, Argyll.

The Mightiest Conifer in Europe

The silver fir *(Abies alba)* is a native of central Europe, the Alps and the Pyrenees. The species was introduced into the United Kingdom about the beginning of the 17th century and the earliest trees recorded are two mentioned by Evelyn as "being planted by Serjeant Newdigate in Harefield Park in 1603".[1] Although mountains are its natural environment, the species thrives throughout the UK.

This specimen is thought to be more than 250 years old, and even in 1881 it was recorded as a huge tree. Mr Wilkie, the estate forester, calculated that it contained 57 tons (56 tonnes) of timber and said that "no true conception of this noble tree can be formed from reading a description of it".[2]

About 1910, after a visit by Charles Sargent, once dubbed "the greatest living authority on trees", Niall Diarmid Campbell (10th Duke of Argyll) wrote to the daughter of the owner of Ardkinglas saying: "It is undeniably the mightiest conifer, if not the biggest bole, of any kind in Europe." Indeed, with a girth of 31 feet (9.4 metres), this colossal silver fir tends to stop people in their tracks.

In 1906 the eminent botanist H J Elwes said that he had "never seen anything surpassing it in bulk, even in the virgin forests of Bosnia".[3] This magnificent silver fir is still thriving and will probably continue growing for many years to come.

Ardkinglas Woodland Garden at Cairndow, Argyll, off the A83 Loch Lomond to Inveraray road on the eastern shores of Loch Fyne. The garden is open all year during daylight hours. Admission charges apply.

Robert The Bruce's Yew

On private land near Tarbet, Argyll.

erched on a rocky outcrop on the western shore of Loch Lomond is an ancient yew *(Taxus baccata)* associated with King Robert the Bruce. Legend has it that The Bruce took shelter from pursuing enemies under the evergreen canopy, entertaining his troops with tales of valour. Bruce and 200 of his followers welcomed the rest, having spent a whole night and day ferrying themselves across the loch in a single leaky rowing boat which could only hold three men at a time. [1]

J C Loudon (1783 – 1843), the influential Scottish writer who chronicled changes in garden design in the early part of the 19th century, paid a visit to The Bruce's yew on his travels. In 1837 he recorded the girth of the trunk at ground level to be 13 feet (4 metres) and the height at 39 feet (12 metres). By 1998 the girth had increased to 20 feet (6.1 metres) and the height reduced to 18 feet (5.5 metres) as a result of heavy pruning in the interim. This suggests an annual ring width of two millimetres, a reasonable rate of increment for a slow-growing species in such a harsh environment. Now past its prime, this old campaigner must be a mere shadow of its former self, yet new sprouts of fresh growth bode well for its future.

A 1920s postcard shows the tree with Loch Lomond in the background.

Inchmahome Veterans

The 13th century priory of Inchmahome, once home to a small community of Augustinian canons, nestles on a small, low-lying island in the middle of the Lake of Mentieth in Stirlingshire. Of the many fine trees on the island, the three veteran sweet chestnuts *(Castanea sativa)* steal the show in terms of antiquity and character. These heavily gnarled individuals are probably more than 400 years old. Although extensively decayed and hollow, they are still very much alive, and are the island's oldest living residents. The girth of their gnarled trunks ranges from 14 feet 4 inches (4.4 metres) to 19 feet 8 inches (6 metres). The largest of the three is known as the 'Antlered Chestnut' because the stag-headed branches resemble the antlers of a deer. [1]

The trees might well have been around when Mary, Queen of Scots paid a visit to the island in 1547. Accompanied by her mother, Mary of Guise, the four-year-old infant queen sought refuge at the priory for three weeks following the English victory at the Battle of Pinkie. A poem penned by the Reverend W M Stirling in 1815 recalls the royal visit:

> " *Those giant boughs that wave around*
>   *My aged hoary head,*
>   *Were then the tenants of the ground*
>   *Where walked the royal maid.* "

Alongside one of the walks radiating from Inchmahome Priory on an island in the Lake of Mentieth, Stirlingshire. The Priory is in the care of Historic Scotland and public access is available via a small passenger ferry most of the year, except the winter months.

The Clachan Oak

The ancient sessile oak *(Quercus petraea)* that stands in Balfron, Stirlingshire is clearly a very old tree of some significance, and forms an interesting focal point. It once occupied the central green of an ancient hamlet known as 'The Clachan', which was ultimately to grow into the village of Balfron.

The tree was recorded in 1867 as being in a 'flourishing condition', with a girth of 15 feet 9 inches (4.8 metres) at 6 feet (1.8 metres) above the ground. At that time it was thought to be 334 years old and to have been struck by lightning 40 years before.[1] The short trunk, which is completely hollow, now measures 16 feet (4.9 metres) in girth.

The Clachan House and Clachan Oak, Balfron.

An Edwardian postcard of the tree.

The most notable features of the tree are the three iron hoops that encircle its trunk. Nowadays they play a useful role in holding the hollow shell together, but originally they had a darker function. Until the end of the 18th century it was common practice to chain petty criminals to the oak tree, where they were subjected to merciless public ridicule. An iron collar was attached around the neck of the unfortunate victims and connected by a length of chain to the iron hoop encircling the trunk of the oak. This form of ritual humiliation was known as 'the jougs', and must have been a most unpleasant form of punishment.

On a small area of public open space next to the Church of Scotland and the A875 road in Balfron, Stirlingshire. Free public access is available throughout the year.

The King Tree

This sweet chestnut (*Castanea sativa*) is a well known resident of a 1950s housing estate, and shows that heritage trees can turn up in the most unlikely places. Known locally as the 'King Tree', it is probably more than 400 years old and once adorned the grounds of 16th century Herbertshire Castle.

The castle grounds were known to be extremely picturesque, with verdant meadows which contained many trees. These beautiful grounds were originally used as a royal hunting station, and it is perhaps this association that is remembered in the tree's name.

Although the castle has long since been demolished, the tree survives as a living relic of a bygone era. The lone chestnut, affectionately referred to by its regal title, has become something of a local landmark within its new suburban surroundings.

Its heavily gnarled trunk is huge, with a girth of 27 feet 3 inches (8.3 metres), one of the largest of its species recorded in Scotland. Despite poor treatment in the past, the gaunt, battered crown of the 'King Tree' is still very much alive, its sparse framework of branches producing a fresh flush of foliage each spring.

An area of council-owned public open space at Chestnut Crescent, Dunipace, Falkirk. Free public access is available.

The Strathleven House Oak

A superb veteran of great character, this tree boasts the largest trunk so far recorded for pendunculate oak (*Quercus robur*) in Scotland, with a girth of 29 feet (8.9 metres). It is probably one of the oldest oaks in Scotland, being several centuries in age. The huge trunk is very decayed and hollow, and the imposing girth is exaggerated by many swellings and burrs. Crudely cut at around 10 feet (3 metres) from ground level many years ago, this old hulk still survives, producing healthy new growth from the cut stumps. It is, however, rather squat and dumpy in appearance, being no more than 46 feet (14 metres) high.

The tree stands hidden within a small copse of woodland some 110 yards (100 metres) from Strathleven House, which now forms part of the Vale of Leven Industrial Estate. Strathleven House was built in 1700 for William Cochrane of Kilmarnock, the Commissioner to Parliament for Renfrew. It is likely that the oak predates the house and was incorporated into its policies, where it must have formed an impressive feature in the landscape.

This wonderful survivor of a bygone age was only recently re-discovered, having been engulfed by a plantation of conifers for over 30 years. Work is now underway to gradually remove some of these encroaching youngsters and give the old oak a new lease of life.

Shortly before going to press, the Strathleven Oak fell victim to vandals. A fire was set in the hollow interior of the trunk, which weakened the structure until the entire tree collapsed. The burned out shell lies prostrate and exhibits no signs of life – a regrettable and ignominious end for one of the oldest and largest oaks in Scotland, and a stark reminder of the ongoing threats faced by many of our heritage trees.

Hidden from view in a small copse, about 90 yards (100 metres) south east of Strathleven House. The grounds are now part of the Vale of Leven Industrial Estate, off the A813 road between Dumbarton and Alexandria. Public access is available.

The Pollok Park Beech

The grossly distorted trunk of this beech *(Fagus sylvatica)* never ceases to amaze visitors. The trunk consists of a swollen and heavily gnarled mass of burrs and branches that appear to have amalgamated through time to form a huge, contorted ball extending from ground level up to 9 feet 10 inches (3 metres). From this massive structure a number of relatively small limbs radiate in all directions to form a low, spreading crown. The trunk is of huge proportions, measuring 23 feet (7 metres) in girth at ground level and expanding to 32 feet 10 inches (10 metres) at its widest point.

Thought to be about 250 years old, this eccentric of the arboricultural world has become a well known focal point in Glasgow's Pollok Park, where it stands atop a small podium in the gardens behind Pollok House. How this prominent tree assumed its outlandish shape is open to conjecture. Perhaps some genetic aberration, coupled with repeated pruning over a long period, might explain its strange form.

The lands of Pollok have been held by the Maxwell family for 700 years. Major plantings by the seventh baronet, Sir John Maxwell (1768 – 1844) and the tenth baronet, Sir John Stirling Maxwell (1866 – 1956), have created a wonderful treescape and lasting legacy for the people of Glasgow.

In the gardens behind Pollok House, Glasgow.
Free public access is available throughout year.

The Arran Whitebeams

The Isle of Arran is home to two species of tree which do not occur anywhere else in the world, the Arran whitebeam *(Sorbus arranensis)* and the Arran cut-leaved whitebeam *(Sorbus pseudofennica)*. They are also Scotland's rarest native trees, and in global terms are officially classed as dangerously close to extinction by the WWF.

Only a few hundred trees of each species exist, clinging perilously to the steep rocky slopes of two remote glens at the north of the island. The Arran whitebeam was first recorded in 1897 and is thought to have arisen as a natural hybrid between the rock whitebeam *(Sorbus rupicola)* and the ubiquitous rowan *(Sorbus aucuparia)*. The other rare hybrid, the Arran cut-leaved whitebeam, was first noted in 1952. This appears to have arisen from the Arran whitebeam back-crossing with the rowan. Both species were more abundant in the past, but have been forced to retreat to their restricted enclaves as the island was progressively improved for agriculture.

Small, windswept and stunted, these uniquely Scottish trees are under constant threat from the strong gales and heavy snow storms common in their montane habitat, as the fragile root systems are easily dislodged from the rocky soil.

Sorbus pseudofennica.

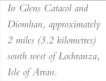

In Glens Catacol and Diomhan, approximately 2 miles (3.2 kilometres) south west of Lochranza, Isle of Arran.

Above: *Sorbus arranensis*.

Opposite: A view of Glen Diomhan reveals
the precarious location of these whitebeams.

The Kelburn Weeping Larch

This outlandish specimen of European larch *(Larix decidua)* in the grounds of Kelburn Castle bears no resemblance to the elegant and graceful form normally associated with the species. Said to have been planted about 1800, the 'weeping larch' occupies a prime position in the castle gardens, which overlook the Firth of Clyde south of Largs, North Ayrshire.

The tree sports a mass of twisting and contorted branches, many of considerable size, which radiate from the short, squat bole and weep to the ground. They proceed to grow haphazardly along the surface for many metres, arching and twisting and throwing up new shoots as they go. Several branches have successfully layered to produce new trees, which in turn are starting to weep and layer, thereby perpetuating the process. Increasing in ever-expanding circles of serpentine branches, this one tree covers almost half an acre.

A fascinating old tree, the Kelburn larch is undoubtedly a mutant monster of the arboricultural world, and probably unique in Britain. However, it is not without considerable character and charm, and is well worth a visit to marvel at its crazy architecture and relentless survival strategy.

Next to the walled garden, or 'Plaisance', of Kelburn Castle, off the A78 road about 1 mile (1.6 kilometres) south of Largs, North Ayrshire. The grounds are managed as a country park and are open to the public for most of the year.

Stevenson's Yew

The famous Scottish author, Robert Louis Stevenson (1850 – 1894), spent part of his childhood with his maternal grandfather at Colinton Manse, Edinburgh. He is known to have played in the spreading branches of the old yew tree *(Taxus baccata)* in the garden. The remains of his swing are still evident on one of the limbs. Stevenson fondly recalls his early days at the manse in the company of the ancient tree:

> *"A yew, which is one of the glories of the village. Under the circuit of its wide, black branches, it was always dark and cool, and there was a green scurf over all the trunk among which glistened the round, bright drops of resin."* [1]

The tree also provided inspiration for his poetry:

> *"Below the yew – it still is there –*
> *Our phantom voices haunt the air*
> *As we were still at play,*
> *And I can hear them call and say,*
> *'How far is it to Babylon?'"* [2]

The tree is thought to be several centuries old and is recorded in the Kirk Session minutes of 1630. It is a fine specimen, with the trunk measuring 12 feet (3.6 metres) in girth. Despite losing some of its lower branches, the yew still stands today, a living link with one of Scotland's great literary figures.

R L Stevenson aged 39

In the private garden of Colinton Manse, Dell Road, Edinburgh.

The Newbattle Abbey Sycamore

This fine sycamore *(Acer pseudoplatanus)* grows in the grounds of Newbattle Abbey, on the outskirts of Dalkeith. It is reputedly the oldest example of the species in Scotland, and perhaps in the UK, and is thought to have been planted around 1550, it is an imposing tree, dominating the front of the house.

In 1904 the tree was recorded as being in good health with a full, billowing crown. It had then reached a height of 98 feet (30 metres) and its trunk measured 16 feet (4.9 metres) in girth [1]. However, it is now showing signs of age and natural decline, and the crown is becoming noticeably stag-headed. When measured in 2003, its height had reduced to 82 feet (25 metres) and the trunk had only gained an extra 2 feet (0.6 metres) in girth.

Many of the oldest and largest sycamores in the UK can be found in the grounds of country houses in Scotland. Originally known as 'plane', sycamore was probably brought to Scotland direct from France during the time of the Reformation in the mid-16th century. Suited to the Scottish climate and soils, it soon became a common feature of the woodland and parkland on many estates. This 'Auld Alliance' between the two countries, has certainly left a rich legacy of wonderful trees.

The tree as depicted in
*The Trees of Great
Britain and Ireland*
by Elwes and Henry
(1906-1913)

*To the front of Newbattle Abbey, Dalkeith, Midlothian.
The abbey now functions as a private adult residential
college. Access with permission only.*

Early woodcut of John Knox,
from Beza's *Icones* (1580)

The Great Yew
of Ormiston

This is a first-class example of the few 'layering' yews *(Taxus baccata)* known in Scotland. Weeping branches radiate out from the solid central trunk and take root where they touch the ground, encircling the tree in an ever-extending fringe of growth. The inner 'chamber' formed by the layered branches and dense foliage creates a spacious, natural cathedral of arching limbs. The huge central trunk measures 22 feet 10 inches (6.9 metres) in girth. Records of measurement over the past 160 years suggest a very slow rate of increment, and it is perfectly feasible that the tree could be as old as 1000 years.

As early as the fifteenth century the yew was recognised as a local landmark: a parchment dated 1474, found among some old papers belonging to the Earl of Hopetoun, had been signed under the yew tree. [1]

The famous religious reformer, John Knox (c. 1514 – 1572), who was born in nearby Haddington, is also reputed to have preached his early sermons within the secluded interior of the yew's evergreen canopy. Here Knox, along with his influential mentor, George Wishart, sowed the seeds of the Reformation which was ultimately to sweep throughout Scotland.

In a private residential development close to the ruins of Ormiston Hall, Ormiston, East Lothian. It is reached from the A6093.

Rizzio's Chestnut

Melville Castle was frequented by Mary, Queen of Scots. During one of her visits, David Rizzio, her Italian secretary and close companion, is said to have planted a tree as a token of his love for her by the banks of the River North Esk. The tree, an ancient sweet chestnut *(Castanea sativa)*, survives to this day next to the stable block, now known appropriately as 'Chestnut House'.

However, such blatant displays of love were to be Rizzio's downfall. He was murdered before the Queen's eyes in the Palace of Holyrood House in 1566 by a group of conspirators led by Mary's jealous second husband, Lord Darnley. Rizzio's chestnut remains today as an enduring symbol of his ill-fated affection for Mary.

The tree is a fine old specimen of huge girth, and it is quite feasible that it did indeed originate in the mid-1560s. The vast trunk is 25 feet (7.6 metres) in girth. Like all ancient sweet chestnuts, it is of no significant height and has died back to 55 feet (16.7 metres). The crown is of reasonable shape, although abundant deadwood indicates that it is in the natural process of decline. However, the capacity for the species to regenerate itself by forming a new crown from dormant buds should guarantee its presence for a few more centuries at least.

In the private garden of Chestnut House, about 110 yards (100 metres) south west of Melville Castle, near Dalkeith, Midlothian. Access is available only with written permission.

The Capon Tree

The Capon Tree, a hollow English oak
(Quercus robur), is one of the last survivors
of the ancient Jed Forest. About 800 years old,
this celebrated tree has been a constant feature
in the turbulent history of the border country.
The origin of the tree's name is uncertain, but
it could have been derived from the word
'capuche', the hood worn by the monks who
sheltered under its branches on their way to the
nearby Jedburgh Abbey.

According to tradition, border clans rallied
for action at the tree during the troubled days
of the 16th century. Living in a border town,
Jedburgh's local families were involved in
fighting the English, and the Jethart Callants
had a reputation for outstanding bravery. Both
they and the Capon Tree are celebrated
annually at the Jedburgh Callants' Festival. Each
July 'The Callant' – a young man chosen to
represent the town – leads his mounted
cavalcade on historic rides, the most important
being to Redeswire to commemorate the last
cross-border skirmish. On Festival Day, the
Callant visits Ferniehurst Castle and on his
return home stops at the Capon Tree, taking a
sprig and wearing it in the lapel of his jacket.

An Edwardian
postcard of the
tree, viewed
from the other
side.

On the banks of the River Jed and alongside the A68 less than 2 miles (3 kilometres) south of Jedburgh town centre, accessible by a 15-minute walk from the town on pavements all the way, starting from the first bridge (near the Abbey). The tree is around the corner on the right just after the third bridge.

The Kailzie Larch

The oldest surviving European larches *(Larix decidua)* in Britain date from 1725, when some of the trees were introduced to a few Peeblesshire estates by Sir James Naesmyth (1644 – 1754), Laird of Posso and Dawyck.

One of the finest specimens can be found at Kailzie Gardens, near Peebles. The larch's introduction to the estate is amusingly recounted by a member of the Innerleithen Alpine Club following a visit to the estate in 1890:

" In 1725, on returning from London, Sir James brought with him in his carriage some young larches, and he called in passing and dined with his friend the Laird of Kailzie. This Laird of Posso and Dawyck, like his father 'The Deil', had trees on the brain and no doubt over the wine waxed eloquent about the new importation. The result was that one specimen was planted next morning in Kailzie Park, and is still standing there, growing vigorously and without symptom of decay. Its height is 105 feet and its circumference four feet from the ground is twelve feet." [1]

The straight, unblemished trunk now measures 15 feet 9 inches (4.8 metres) girth at 4 feet (1.2 metres) above the ground, a respectable increase of 3 feet 9 inches (1.1 metres) since 1890. It supports a crown that has developed huge, up-curved limbs typically seen in many old larches.

Kailzie Garden, off the B7062 road about 3 miles (4.8 kilometres) south east of Peebles, Scottish Borders. The garden is open to the public seven days a week throughout the year.

Rabbie Burns' Sycamore

The fine, large sycamore *(Acer pseudoplatanus)* that dominates Alloway Auld Kirk, built in 1516, has taken the name of Scotland's National Bard. Robert Burns (1759 – 1796), who was born a stone's throw from the kirk, was inspired by this eerie setting and later immortalised the kirk in his famous work, 'Tam O' Shanter':

> *"When, glimmering through the groaning trees,*
> *Kirk-Alloway seem'd in a bleeze,*
> *Through ilka bore the beams were glancing,*
> *And loud resounding mirth and dancing."*

The grand and imposing sycamore, which appears to emerge from the foundations of the ancient kirk, certainly adds to the atmosphere. The shapely, spreading crown is 74 feet (22.5 metres) tall and the single, squat trunk has a girth of 12 feet 6 inches (3.8 metres). At some time in the past the church wall has been carefully bridged over the swollen root buttresses to accommodate its ever-increasing girth. Its date of origin and provenance is unknown, although judging by its dimensions, it probably began growing in the 18th century.

It is tempting to imagine that this gentle giant that now watches over 'Alloway's Auld Haunted Kirk' was around when the young Burns began writing poems inspired by the natural world around him.

Next to the ruins of Alloway Auld Kirk, in the village of Alloway on the southern outskirts of Ayr, South Ayrshire. Free public access is available throughout the year.

Blairquhan Dool Tree

A 'dool' or 'dule' tree was once used as a natural gallows for hanging criminals. They were common features on many estates until the middle of the 18th century. Such trees normally occupied a prominent location near the laird's residence, where the corpse was left to swing as a deterrent for all to see. The favoured species used for this purpose was sycamore, because its strong and resilient timber was unlikely to fail at the crucial moment. The name 'dool' derives from old Scots and means sorrowful or mournful.

One of Scotland's few surviving dool trees is the ancient sycamore *(Acer pseudoplatanus)* that stands in the shadow of Blairquhan Castle, near Straiton, Ayrshire. The tree is thought to have been planted about 1500 during the reign of James V of Scotland. The moss-covered trunk has a girth of 18 feet 4 inches (5.6 metres) and is completely hollow, with only a very thin outer shell of sound wood supporting the tree. The once spreading crown was heavily pruned in 1997 in an effort to preserve the fragile shell and prevent the much-weakened trunk from total collapse. Vigorous new growth is now establishing a new, smaller crown. This unwitting instrument of execution will remain in the land of the living for a while yet.

Close to Blairquhan House, Blairquhan estate, off the B741 road about 1 mile (1.6 kilometres) west of Straiton, South Ayrshire. The house and grounds are open to the public during the last two weeks of July and the first two weeks of August, or by appointment. Admission charges apply.

The Lochwood Oaks

A small stand of ancient sessile oaks *(Quercus petraea)* lies close to Lochwood Tower, near Moffat, Dumfries and Galloway. These trees are the surviving remnants of a long-established oak forest dating back many centuries, and include individuals of great age and character. This valuable population of veteran trees now supports an important range of wildlife and lichens.

During the 1970s, the trees at Lochwood played an important role in the development of dendrochronology: the study of annual rings to date wooden artefacts and past events. As a tree grows, it puts on an annual growth ring. Because trees grow at different rates according to the weather, they have wider rings in favourable years and narrower rings in unfavourable years. Sequences of tree-rings thus give unique patterns which reflect changes in climate over a long period of time. The ring sequence, taken as a core sample, also provides a unique 'fingerprint' which can be detected in other trees growing in the same geographical area.

The old oaks at Lochwood allowed scientists to construct a ring sequence from 1571 to 1970. Once this tree ring sequence had been established, timbers in local buildings could be compared to the sequence, providing accurate dates for when the building was constructed. This technique has proved so useful that many universities and laboratories around the world are currently establishing their own tree ring sequences to aid in the dating of wood.

Lochwood Castle, near Moffat, Dumfries and Galloway.
The site is an SSSI and public access is limited.

The Wesley Beeches

Belying initial appearances, here are two beech trees (*Fagus sylvatica*) which have grafted together to form a single entity. Over the years the union between the two has become so grossly swollen and contorted that it is now difficult to tell where one tree ends and the other begins. Despite the outlandish appearance of the knotted trunks, the combined crown is of considerable size and appears healthy and vigorous.

However, this exceptional growth is no accident of nature. It is the living result of action by John Wesley (1703 – 91), the founding father of Methodism, who twined two saplings together in 1787 to represent the unity of Methodism and Anglicanism [1].

John Wesley and his younger brother Charles (1707 – 88) began preaching their religious message of repentance, faith and love around 1738. This did not find acceptance with the established Anglican church of the time and they were forced to organise their own societies and conduct their meetings out of doors. They had many working class converts, whose spiritual needs the Wesleys felt had been neglected by the established church.

John was a tireless worker and travelled the country on horseback preaching thousands of sermons, many under the sheltering boughs of trees (see The Pulpit Yew, page 170). On a mission to the mills of Lambeg, in the industrial Laggan Valley on the outskirts of Lisburn, he stayed with his friends the Wolfenden family at Chrome Hill. It was during this visit that Wesley joined together the pair of beeches which still stand today as a living reminder of his message.

In the private garden of a house known as 'Chrome Hill', on the Ballyskeagh Road at Lambeg, near the City of Lisburn.
The trees are readily visible from the main road and public footpath.

The Original Irish Yew

The compact, upright form of the Irish yew (*Taxus baccata* 'fastigiata') is instantly recognisable, and is a common feature of many churchyards and gardens throughout the UK. A naturally occurring female variant of the common yew (*Taxus baccata*), this variety owes its existence to a random freak of nature and a sharp-eyed farmer. Some time around 1770, while hunting in the Cuileagh Mountains of Fermanagh, George Willis, a tenant of the Earl of Enniskillen, came across two yews with an unusual upright habit. Intrigued by their unfamiliar shape, he carefully lifted them from their niche next to Carrig-na-madadh (Rock of the Dog) and carried them down the slopes to his farm. He planted one of the seedlings on his own land and dutifully gifted the other to his landlord, who planted it out in the grounds of the family estate at Florence Court.

Unfortunately for Willis, his specimen died in 1865, while the Earl's tree flourished. The unique growth habit of tightly upswept branches soon began to attract attention from the horticultural fraternity and propagated cuttings from the tree became commercially available from around 1820. The new variety, known originally as the 'Florence Court Yew' after its place of origin, was widely planted throughout the 19th century.

The Earl's original tree survives to this day, the progenitor of all the other Irish yews in existence, and many of its early offspring can be found scattered throughout the extensive demesne of Florence Court. It is, however, showing signs of its age: the crown has lost some of its shape and is becoming rather open and scrappy. Perhaps this is not surprising, given the hard life that this mother tree has had producing so many millions.

The tree is in the care of the Northern Ireland Forest Service and stands within the Florence Court Forest Park, off the A32 approximately 7 miles (11 kilometres) south of Enniskillen, Co Fermanagh. A network of well-marked footpaths leads to the tree.
The yew can also be accessed from the National Trust property of Florence Court. There is free public access to the tree throughout the year.

The Great Yews at Crom

Regarded as among the most impressive trees in Northern Ireland, this huge 'tree' is actually two yews *(Taxus baccata)* – one male, one female – thought to have been planted close together in the 17th century. They are situated near the ruins of the old Crom Castle, which has stood guard over the narrowest point of Lough Erne since 1610. By the latter half of the 19th century they were said to "resemble an enormous green mushroom in contour." [1]

Originally the trees' branches were supported by 32 brick pillars. These were replaced in 1833 by a series of oak posts with their bark on [2]. It was even said that at its "formal peak", the 'tree' covered an area about 75 feet (23 metres) across and that a party of 200 often dined under it. [3]

Over time the oak posts were lost and the 'tree' developed a less formal state, reverting to a more natural rambling condition. The land where the Great Yews now stand is part of the National Trust holding. The current Lord Erne still lives on the estate in "new" Crom Castle and maintains great affection for this fantastic 'tree'.

The female Crom Castle Yew (above),
and the male tree (main picture).

By boat: Crom is next to the Shannon-Erne Waterway and north east of Crichton Tower. Public jetty at Visitor Centre. By road: Crom is well signposted from the A34 at Newtownbutler and Lisnaskea or from the N54 between Clones and Cavan. It is located just 3 miles (5 kilometres) west of the village of Newtownbutler. The estate opens April to September daily 10 am to 8 pm (Sundays 12 noon to 8 pm).

The Crom
Castle Yews,
as they appeared
in the early
20th century.

The Borrowdale Yew

Detail of one of the fraternal Four.

estling under the Cumbrian fells, this ancient yew is the largest survivor of the yews *(Taxus baccata)* which Wordsworth celebrated in his 1803 poem, *Yew Trees*, as "those fraternal Four of Borrowdale."

> " *But worthier still of note*
> *Are those fraternal Four of Borrowdale,*
> *Joined in one solemn and capacious grove;*
> *Huge trunks! and each particular trunk a growth*
> *Of intertwisted fibres serpentine*
> *Up-coiling, and inveterately convolved* "

The 'fraternal Four' lost one of their number in the great storm of 1883 and F A Malleson wrote in 1886: "The Borrowdale Yews have sustained serious injury from winter storms especially those of 1883-4, but even in their wrecked condition they are worth a visit." [1]

The three surviving trees, and the remains of the fourth, are now owned by the National Trust. This female tree is hollow, with enough space in its trunk for four people to squeeze inside. Over the years, unfortunately, people have lit fires in the hollow interior, but luckily the tree still thrives and hopefully will continue to do so for many more centuries.

Take the B5289 from Keswick towards Buttermere. Turn left at Seatoller, taking the minor road to Seathwaite. Park at Seathwaite Farm. Cross over the field to the west of the car park and turn right. The tree can be found 200 yards (180 metres) further on.

Great Lime at Holker

One of the largest and finest common limes in Britain, this awe-inspiring tree *(Tilia x europaea)* has an enormous fluted trunk. Common lime is a hybrid between small-leaved and large-leaved limes, which appears to have arisen naturally. The date of its introduction to Britain is uncertain. The tree's girth is 25 feet 11 inches (7.9 metres) and it is an amazing sight to behold.

The lime grows in the 25-acre gardens of Holker Hall, an impressive building owned by Lord Cavendish, which is surrounded by a deer park planted in the late 18th century by Lord George Cavendish. The earliest records of a house on the present site date back to the beginning of the 16th century. From then until the present day the estate has been the home of three families: the Prestons, the Lowthers and the Cavendishes. The estate has never been bought or sold, but has passed by inheritance through the family line.

It is thought that the "Great Lime" was probably planted as part of the establishment of the formal gardens in the early 17th century. The earliest record of the Holker gardens dates back to the 1720s when Sir Thomas Lowther and Lady Elizabeth Cavendish were the owners. The gardens are now a beautiful setting and include several other record trees including some spectacular monkey puzzles.

Take the A590 north west from M6 junction 36 (South Lakes). Holker Hall is then well signposted. Walk through the "Formal Gardens" and follow the path to the right of the Meadow for 150 yards (140 metres). The Great Lime is on the right, behind the wrought iron circular seat.

Umbrella Tree at Levens Hall

The topiary gardens as depicted in the *Gardeners' Chronicle* (1874).

The topiary gardens at Levens Hall are world famous as the finest and earliest collection of topiary in Britain, comprising over 100 topiary shapes and an extensive beech hedge. Topiary is the art of training and clipping trees and shrubs into geometric, intricate or fanciful shapes. The gardens were laid out in 1694, after Colonel Grahme came to live at Levens. He was friendly with John Evelyn (1620 - 1706), the author of *Silva*, who encouraged him to create a formal garden and Grahme engaged a Monsieur Guillaume Beaumont to design it.

The Umbrella Tree, the largest yew *(Taxus baccata)* in the gardens, is thought to be about 400 years old and may predate the creation of the formal gardens in 1694. It reaches a height of 29 feet 6 inches (9 metres) and has a girth of 6 feet 3 inches (1.9 metres). Keeping topiary in shape is a skilled, time-consuming process and a team of gardeners works on the trees from mid-October until December every year. Amazingly, in the 300 or so years since the gardens were established, there have been only ten head gardeners.

Levens Hall is situated 5 miles (8 kilometres) south of Kendal off the A6 and is only 5 minutes drive north west from M6 junction 36. The gardens are open Sundays to Thursdays mid-April until mid-October from 10 am until 5 pm (last entry 4.30pm). Admission charges apply.

Wild Cherry
at Studley Royal

Britain's largest wild cherry *(Prunus avium)* can be found in the grounds of Studley Royal Deer Park, part of the Studley estate which John Aislabie inherited in 1693. He became the Tory Member of Parliament for Ripon in 1695 and in 1718 became Chancellor of the Exchequer.

In 1720 Aislabie was a principal sponsor of the South Sea Company scheme and its collapse (the South Sea Bubble) saw him expelled from Parliament and disqualified for life from public office.

Aislabie returned to Yorkshire and devoted himself to the creation of a garden. After his death in 1742, his son William extended his scheme and between them they created what is arguably England's most important 18th century water garden.

In 1983 the estate was acquired by the National Trust. The deer park, the oldest feature of the estate, was already well established when John Aislabie came into his inheritance. It has had many uses since medieval times and the 360 acre (146 hectare) park is still grazed today by 500 red, sika and fallow deer.

The Studley Royal Wild Cherry measures 18 feet 8 inches (5.7 metres) in girth and is a stunning sight, especially when flowering in the spring. It is one of the highlights of the deer park (which has many other ancient trees), dominating its location and well in keeping with its 'World Heritage Site' backdrop.

Take the B6265 from Ripon towards Pateley Bridge. Turn left into Studley Royal and at the bottom continue into the park. Go straight on to the cross-roads, then turn right and after approximately 50 yards (45 metres) the tree is on the right.

The Marton Oak

Late 19th century photograph of the tree.

This enormous sessile oak (*Quercus petraea*) is now four separate parts which together have a girth of 44 feet (13.4 metres). Nearly 200 years ago Daniel and Samuel Lyson, in their survey of Cheshire, recorded that "not far from the Chapel is a very fine oak, believed to be the largest in England." [1] This 'little known' champion among oaks was measured then at 43 feet (13 metres) in circumference, 4 feet (1.2 metres) from the base. It was referred to in 1880 as the largest tree in England and it may still be. It grows in the garden of a private house in Marton village and, over the years, has served variously as a bullpen, a pigsty and a Wendy house.

The tree is still productive and at the centre of village life. Acorns from the tree are collected by children from the school and have helped raise funds for the ancient church nearby, which is the earliest longitudinal timber church in Europe. The oak also features on the village sign and is the much-loved focus of Marton parish.

Growing in private grounds, the Marton Oak can be viewed by appointment. Visiting arrangements can be made by contacting the Tree Council (Phone: 020 7407 9992).

The Major Oak

This vast hollow English oak *(Quercus robur)* is about 35 feet (11 metres) in girth and its leaves and branches spread 92 feet (28 metres). It grows in Sherwood Forest and is famous because it is said to have associations with Robin Hood. However, the tree first became well known after it was described in 1790 by a local historian, Major Hayman Rooke, from whom it takes its name. Rooke, a noted antiquary, described most of the ancient oaks of Nottinghamshire and wrote a book about the oaks of Welbeck.[1] Before Rooke's time the tree was known as the Cockpen Tree, since "a breed of game cocks used the tree as a roosting place."[2] Throughout the 19th century it was also known as the Queen or Queen's Oak.

Because of its fame, the tree has been propped up and supported over the years to prevent wide-spreading branches from falling off. It is now fenced to protect the roots from trampling. Much photographed throughout the 20th century, it is the most common tree image on early postcards (two of which are illustrated here). It is now owned by Nottinghamshire County Council and is probably the most famous tree in Britain. Despite its more recent status as an ancient monument, the Major Oak is still a remarkable wildlife habitat and can be regarded as a nature reserve in its own right.

From the A614 at Ollerton, take the A6075 to the village of Edwinstowe and the B6034 to Sherwood Forest Country Park & Visitor Centre. The Major Oak is approximately 15 minutes walk from the Visitor Centre.

The Original Bramley

A Bramley's Seedling apple from the tree at Southwell.

This tree, the original Bramley apple tree, was grown from a pip planted by a young Mary Ann Brailsford between 1809 and 1815. The pip is thought to have come from an apple tree in her garden and grew into a fine seedling which was planted out and bore its first fruit in 1837. Twenty years later, a local nurseryman, Henry Merryweather, recognised the apple as an excellent variety and asked Mr Bramley, the then owner of the tree, for permission to take cuttings. Mr Bramley agreed but insisted that it should bear his name – hence 'Bramley's Seedling' when it really should have been called 'Brailsford's Seedling'!

The tree then became neglected and in about 1900 it fell over but, as it remained rooted, it continued to grow and produced new roots where the trunk touched the ground – an example of a 'Phoenix tree' in ancient tree terminology. When the current owner acquired the tree in the 1970s it was in a very neglected condition. A nurseryman, the late Claude Coates, restored it to better health.

Nottingham University recently cloned the tree and a new specimen is now growing in the garden. The original tree is still producing heavy crops of Bramley apples – the variety generally accepted as the world's best cooking apple. There are now 500 Bramley apple growers in the country and the total UK market is worth around £50 million. Amazingly, it all began with a single pip.

Growing in private grounds at Southwell, Nottinghamshire, the tree can be viewed by appointment. Visiting arrangements can be made by contacting the owner through the Tree Council (Phone: 020 7407 9992).

Woolsthorpe Manor is 7 miles (11 kilometres) south of Grantham, ¹/₂ mile (1 kilometres) north west of Colsterworth, 1 mile (1.5 kilometres) west of A1 (not to be confused with Woolsthorpe near Belvoir). Leave A1 at Colsterworth roundabout and take the B676. At the second crossroads turn right, following National Trust signs.

Newton's Apple Tree

This apple tree at Woolsthorpe Manor, Lincolnshire, is one of the most historically important trees in Britain. It is believed that the tree, which is of the rare variety "Flower of Kent", is where Isaac Newton was sitting in 1665/6 when "the notion of gravitation came into his mind." [1]

The first printed account of Newton's discovery was when Voltaire wrote, "Newton walking in his garden had the first thought of his System of Gravitation, upon seeing an apple fall from a tree." [1]

The link to a particular apple tree has been the subject of much debate. The first mention of a specific tree appears in a book by Edmund Turnor in 1806 who in a footnote stated "The apple tree is now remaining and is showed to strangers." [2] The tree fell over sometime before 1820 but, like the Bramley (see page 90), it appears to have continued growing well, rooting where the trunk touched the ground. Keesing in 1998 [3] came to the conclusion that this tree "is one and the same tree which was identified as the tree from which Newton saw the apple fall."

Whether or not Turnor correctly identified the original tree, there is no doubt that this tree, which has been celebrated for nearly 200 years as Newton's apple tree, is a national treasure.

Bowthorpe
Oak at Bourne

Shaped over the centuries by the prevailing wind, this hollow English oak *(Quercus robur)* at Bowthorpe Park Farm near Bourne in Lincolnshire currently has the largest girth of any English oak in the UK at 42 feet (12.8 metres).

In 1768 George Pauncefoot fitted a floor and benches and the crown was used as a pigeon house. By 1805 it was reported that the tree had been "in the same state of decay" since "the memory of the oldest inhabitants and their ancestors" [1], and that past owners had used the huge hollow trunk as an outdoor eating place, fitting it with a door and seating for 20 people. [1] The original opening has since narrowed, the floor and benches have long since disappeared, but still visible is the graffiti carved into the inside of the tree by previous generations.

Today's proud owner, farmer Richard Blanchard, charges visitors a small fee to see his remarkable tree, which must be more than 1000 years old. In 1999, he told the author that "with the current state of farming, this tree is one of the few things on this farm that make a profit."

Take the A6121 from Stamford towards Bourne. Bowthorpe Park Farm is on the right of the road half a mile (1 kilometre) before the Witham-on-the-Hill crossroads. Park in the farmyard. No appointment needed. A small fee is charged to see the tree.

Ely's London Plane

Bishop Peter Gunning
(1614-1684).

The London plane (*Platanus x hispanica*) is thought to be a hybrid between Oriental (*P. orientalis*) and American plane (*P. occidentalis*), although it may be simply a form of Oriental plane. First noticed in about 1663, it may be that the hybrid cross occurred in the Lambeth garden of the famous 17th century gardener and plant hunter, John Tradescant (1577 - 1638), as both species were growing there.

This particular tree is thought to be one of the first hybrid London planes in Britain and was planted by Bishop Peter Gunning in 1680 in the grounds of the Bishop's Palace, Ely. John Evelyn (author of *Silva*) regularly attended Gunning's services when he preached in London and it is therefore possible that the Bishop sought his advice when choosing the tree.

At the end of the 19th century, Elwes [1] reported that the tree was suffering due to a series of dry seasons, but that "Sir W Thiselton Dyer top-dressed the tree with good soil, and greatly improved the tree's health and vigour."

The London plane copes well with pollution, and this hybrid was therefore planted widely in urban streets and squares, changing forever the treescape of British cities.

The Old Bishop's Palace, now a Sue Ryder Care Home, is in the centre of Ely, on Palace Green, close to the cathedral. On entering Ely by Cambridge Road, leading into St Mary's Street, turn right into the Gallery, keeping the cathedral on the left, and the Old Palace on the right. The garden is open on two days per year, under the National Gardens Scheme: for dates see current edition of the yellow book. Visiting at other times by appointment only (Phone: 01353 667686).

The First Dawn Redwood

rowing in Cambridge University Botanic Garden, Britain's first dawn redwood *(Metasequoia glyptostroboides)* is a fascinating tree, not least because of the way in which the species was discovered. In Japan, during 1941, a paleobotanist called Shigeru Miki was looking at fossil sequoias and he noticed a new fossil genus, which he called "metasequoia" (new sequoia). Amazingly, in the same year, a living tree was found in the Szechuan province of China. Eventually specimens arrived in Beijing in 1946 where Professor Cheng and Dr Hu realised that here was Miki's fossil metasequoia, alive and well, three to five million years after it was thought to have become extinct. [1 and 2]

The Chinese botanists informed Professor Merrill of the Arnold Arboretum of Harvard University about the discovery, and in September 1947 an expedition was sent to Szechuan to bring back seeds. By 1948 the Arnold Arboretum was distributing seed to botanical gardens and collectors around the world. However, the seed from which the specimen at Cambridge was grown came directly from a Dr Silow who worked with the British Council in Beijing. [3] This head start allowed Cambridge University to be the first to plant out a dawn redwood on British soil.

The Cambridge University Botanic Garden is situated 1 mile (1.5 kilometres) south of the city centre, with the entrance on Bateman Street off Trumpington Road (A1134). The Dawn Redwood can be found on the south-western edge of the Lake. The Garden is open all year round and there is a modest admission charge.

Kett's Oak at Hethersett

On 9th July 1549, legend has it that under this English oak (*Quercus robur*), Robert Kett made a rousing speech at the start of the 'Norfolk Rising' against the enclosure of common land. Kett and an army of about 20,000 men marched on Norwich but were defeated. He was imprisoned in the Tower of London, found guilty of treason, and hanged at Norwich Castle.

There is some doubt about whether this is the original Kett's tree, as it appears small for a tree around 500 years old. Norfolk County Council proposed three possible explanations: first, that the tree is very slow growing (as suggested by the analysis of a wood sample); second, that the original tree was destroyed soon after Kett's execution but acorns were saved and planted out; and third, that the existing tree commemorates the place and event and was planted sometime after 1549.

Whichever of these is true, Kett's Oak stands as living memorial and local landmark. Although now propped up it still produces acorns annually. Acorns planted alongside the tree in 1993 by pupils of Hethersett Middle School are flourishing.

Kett the Tanner, seated under the Oak of Reformation, passing his decrees to "The Rebels", wood engraving (1803). This view of the tree, from the other side, shows the distinctive shape of the bole.

Take the A11 from Wymondham, Norfolk, following the signs for the B1135, then turn right at the roundabout. At the second roundabout turn right again onto the B1172 towards Hethersett. After approximately half a mile (1 kilometre), and before the "Hethersett" village sign, park in the lay-by on the left. Kett's Oak is at the Hethersett end of this lay-by.

Hethel Old Thorn is 6 miles (10 kilometres) south west of Norwich. Leave Norwich on the B1113 road to New Buckenham. Turn left into Hethel and head for the church. Limited parking is available on the verge near the church. The Thorn can be found about 330 yards (300 metres) down the public footpath from the church. Access is over a stile.

Hethel Old Thorn

The Hethel Old Thorn grows in a tranquil setting at the edge of a tiny south Norfolk village, near the church. Covering only 0.06 acres (0.025 hectares), the Hethel Old Thorn is one of the smallest nature reserves in the UK. It is a hawthorn (*Crataegus monogyna*) and is thought to be at least 700 years old. Although usually regarded as a short hedge shrub, hawthorn can become a statuesque small tree and can attain great age.

The first written record of the tree appears to be by Marsham who, in a letter to the Bath Society in 1755, made its girth "9 ft. 1 1/4 in. at four feet from the ground; one branch of it extending above 7 yards" [1]. Sir Hugh Beevor in 1895 found it to be "13 feet (around) at 18 inches from the ground where the girth was least" [2].

Elwes records in 1913 that "The branches, which now measure 37 yards round, are sound and covered with leaves and fruit, though bearing many tufts of mistletoe. It is protected from cattle by a rail; and the branches are supported by numerous props" [3].

Veteran hawthorn trees do not retain their bulk as they grow old, and the current girth of the tree is actually smaller than in the past, being nearer to 7 feet (2 metres) [4]. Nevertheless, this ancient and venerable tree is the oldest hawthorn in East Anglia, and probably one of the oldest in the country.

The tree as depicted in *The Trees of Great Britain and Ireland* by Elwes and Henry (1906–13).

Panshanger Great Oak

Wood engraving from
Sylva Britannica by J.G. Strutt (1830).

The largest clear-stemmed oak in the country, the Great Oak is believed to have been planted by Queen Elizabeth I. This ancient English oak *(Quercus robur)* has a well recorded history, including a visit in 1789 by the Hampshire naturalist, Gilbert White (see page 124). It was first measured by Arthur Young in 1804 and then recorded by Strutt in his *Sylva Britannica* in 1830 as being 19 feet (5.8 metres) in circumference 3 feet (0.9 metres) from the ground. Currently its girth is a massive 25 feet (7.6 metres).

Sir Winston Churchill, who planted an oak nearby grown from one of its acorns, described it as the finest and most stately oak growing in the south-east of England.

The tree grows in the grounds of Panshanger House. In 1957 Lady Cowper, the owner of the estate, decreed that when she died her family home should be knocked down so that nobody else could live in it. Her wish was duly carried out.

Panshanger Great Oak is now owned by Lafarge Aggregates, and it was used by English Nature to launch the 'Veteran Tree Initiative' in 1996. It is one of 500 ancient trees in the 1000 acre (400 hectare) estate.

Growing in private grounds in Hertfordshire, the Panshanger Oak can be viewed by appointment. Visiting arrangements can be made by contacting Lafarge Aggregates on 01992 512711.

A riverside Black Poplar, from
The Forest Trees of Britain
by Rev. C.A. Johns.

*Roydon is on the Essex/Herts
border near Harlow. Drive up the
lane leading from the top of the
High Street and park by the
allotments. Take the bridleway on
the left into the open countryside
and after 600 yards (550 metres)
turn left after crossing the stream.
Keep along the field edge for 860
yards (800 metres). The tree is
just before the path reaches a track.
Other black poplars can be seen
on the way.*

World's End Black Poplar

This old pollard is one of 30 rare black poplars (*Populus nigra subsp betulifolia*) growing in the Essex parish of Roydon. These trees are particularly remarkable because they are all female and there are only 600 female black poplars recorded nationwide. Roydon therefore probably has the finest collection in Britain. Native black poplars are beautiful trees but are nationally rare, with a current British population of less than 7,000.

Roydon's first native black poplar was identified during a Tree Council campaign in 1995, when there were only 1500 black poplar trees known in the rest of the country. In 1999 when the Roydon Tree Wardens discovered another 29 females they secured a grant from the Countryside Agency's Local Heritage Initiative to safeguard the future of these veteran pollards.

Children from Roydon School have been involved in studying the trees, including visiting the site, seeing a tree surgeon at work, attending sessions on tree care and identification and learning about uses for black poplar timber. They have also produced a widely acclaimed book based on their work and Alan Burgess, the Tree Warden who worked with the children on the project, has shown his paintings of the tree at various exhibitions.

Take Beeches Road off the A355 in Farnham Common. Straight over at the cross roads into Burnham Beeches (open 8am-dusk) and park. Continue along the road, over a small cross roads. 60 yards (50 metres) past a parking bay for disabled visitors is a path on the right, into a grazing enclosure. The cage pollard is to the right and in front.

Cage Pollard
at Burnham Beeches

Wood engraving from *The Penny Magazine* (1842).

Owned by the Corporation of London, the woods known as Burnham Beeches contain over 450 ancient pollards that are estimated to date back to the 16th century. These trees are all that remain of an estimated 3000 pollards that existed at Burnham in the 17th century. The 'cage pollard' is a very characteristic pollarded beech *(Fagus sylvatica)* that stands within an area of restored wood-pasture. The trunks of all of the old trees are decaying to some degree, but in the 'cage pollard' some strips of the bark and sapwood have also decayed and a series of struts has developed.

In 1990 Burnham Beeches was the location for a major feature film, *Robin Hood Prince of Thieves*. Many scenes were shot there, including a burial scene with the cage pollard as the backdrop. The film was a worldwide success and surprisingly, the tree also became a film star.

Word spread and many visitors went to the Beeches specifically to see the tree. Unfortunately, the ground around it became compacted and, because of its unusual shape, people were tempted to touch and climb on the tree. To protect it, a fence has been erected so that people can view the tree without contributing to its decline.

Ankerwycke Yew at Runnymede

With an estimated age of 2,000 years, this historically important yew (*Taxus baccata*) stands close to the River Thames within sight of "Runeymead" and was a silent witness to the oathing and sealing of the Magna Carta by King John in June 1215. It grows in the grounds of the now ruined Priory of Ankerwycke. Henry VIII is said to have met Anne Boleyn under the tree in the 1530s.

The first documentary record of the tree appears to date from around 1813 when its girth was measured. Strutt then described the tree in detail in 1830 [1]. In 1894 Lowe [2] recorded that it was one of only 31 yews in England and Wales with a girth of over 30 feet (9.1 metres). Currently it has an impressive girth of over 31 feet (9.4 metres).

The tree came to prominence in recent years when the estate was threatened by development proposals, part of which would have been very close to the yew. The efforts of the Ankerwycke Action Group and the Friends of the Ankerwycke Yew resulted in the estate and its famous yew being taken into protection by the National Trust in the spring of 1998.

Take the B376 Staines Road, from M25 junction 13, in a north westerly direction towards Wraysbury. Turn left into Magna Carta Lane. Park at the Ankerwycke Farm buildings. From the information board follow the green waymarkers through the kissing gate in the corner of the field. Keeping the fence line to your left, walk down Poplar Avenue, cross the brick bridge and take the path to the left. The tree can be found about 33 yards (30 metres) further on.

Old Lion Ginkgo at Kew

Ginkgo trees *(Ginkgo biloba)* are the only survivors of a group of plants *(Ginkgoales)* which were widespread 190 million years ago. Thought by some scientists to be the first trees to have evolved, they grew in Britain 60 million years ago. Fossil remains can still be found in Scarborough. About 30 million years ago the species formed extensive stands across the London basin but then disappeared from the native flora as a result of climatic changes.

Ginkgos were brought back to Europe during the 18th century and arrived in Britain in 1754. This tree was the first of the species to be replanted in Britain, originating from seed brought from China and grown in a nursery in the Mile End district of London. The young tree was then sold to the Duke of Argyll for his estate at Twickenham. When he died in 1761 his ginkgo tree was still capable of being moved and it was taken in a barge down to Kew by Lord Bute, for the new arboretum of Princess Augusta. It is still thriving at nearly 250 years old and can be seen by the Wisteria Cage near the Secluded Garden.

Fossil leaves of the Ginkgo – little changed for almost 200 million years.

Kew is situated on the south bank of the River Thames near Richmond, about 6 miles (10 kilometres) south-west of London. The tree can be seen by the Wisteria Cage near the Secluded Garden. Admission charges apply.

Charlton House Mulberry

Introduced into Britain in 1548, the first mulberry trees *(Morus nigra)* were planted at Syon Park, London. In 1608 James I recommended the cultivation of silkworms and offered packets of mulberry seeds to all who would sow them. As a result, mulberry trees became increasingly popular and Loudon said that "there is scarcely an old garden or gentlemen's seat throughout the country, which can be traced back to the 17th century, in which a mulberry tree is not to be found." [1] Unfortunately, the King was promoting black mulberry, when silkworms actually feed on white mulberry *(Morus alba)*.

An old plaque by this tree says "The first Mulberry in England planted in the year 1608 by Order of James I." Although in fact this was not the first mulberry tree planted

in England, it was probably the first planted after the "Order" from King James since it stands in the grounds of Charlton House, in Greenwich, London. The house was built by Adam Newton, tutor to King James's eldest son Prince Henry. It is probable that Newton planted the tree at the start of the King's mulberry promotion. This mulberry is certainly one of the oldest known to be still growing.

The Mulberry can be found in the grounds of Charlton House, now a public park on Charlton Road, Greenwich, London. The tree is behind a red brick toilet block, 30 feet (10 metres) from the park entrance on the left of the path.

Sidney Oak at Penshurst

19th century wood engraving of
The Death of Sir Philip Sidney.

According to legend, the Sidney Oak was planted on 30th November 1554 to celebrate the birth of the soldier and poet Sir Philip Sidney, who served Queen Elizabeth I and was the first commoner to be honoured with a state funeral.

The girth of this English oak (*Quercus robur*) actually suggests an age nearer 1,000 years, which predates Sidney's birth. However, Sir Philip could well have sat beneath its spreading branches while writing his poetry. A description of the tree in the 1794 *Country Gentleman's Magazine* [1] reads: "Within the hollow of it there is a seat and it is capable of containing five or six persons." In 1954 the 1st Viscount De L'Isle wrote: "It is most interesting for us to have confirmation that the tree was as large in 1794 and people could get into the bole."

Vandalism, fire and old age have led to the current perilous condition of the tree. Fortunately in 1998 Dr Tim Marks from Horticulture Research International at The West Malling Research Centre produced a clone of the Sidney Oak which has grown to more than 4 feet (1.2 metres) in four years.

The present Viscount hopes that, once planted alongside the original, the young tree will "still be living in the year 3000."

From M25 junction 5, follow A21 to Tonbridge, Kent, leaving at Hildenborough exit; then follow brown tourist signs to Penshurst Place. Normally open weekends from early March and daily from mid-March until early November 10:30am – 6:00pm. Ask for directions to the tree at the entrance.

The Crowhurst Yew

An Edwardian postcard by F. Frith & Co. Ltd.

A door in this stunning ancient yew *(Taxus baccata)* in Crowhurst churchyard leads into a large hollow trunk. The yew is thought to be 4000 years old, although the first note of the tree's girth dates from an old parish record of 1630, when it was measured at 30 feet (9.1 metres). Evelyn in 1664 recorded that there is a yew "in the churchyard of Crowhurst in the county of Surrey, which I am told is ten yards in compass." [1] Yew enthusiast Allen Meredith measured the girth in 1984 at 31 feet 6 inches (9.6 metres) and therefore in 354 years the tree had grown only 1 foot 6 inches (0.5 metres) in diameter [2].

In 1850, Brailey reported that the hollow inside of the tree had been "fitted up with a table in the centre and benches around." [2] By 1890 the table had gone, but the benches remained [3]. A letter in *The Times* mentioned that a cannonball found in the interior was supposed to have been there since the civil war.

Now the benches are gone but the door remains. Despite its great age the yew is still in good health and has featured in many modern books and articles.

Follow the B2029 towards Lingfield, Surrey from the A22 at Blindley Heath. About $^{1}/_{3}$ mile (0.5 kilometres) along Ray Lane take the first turning left into Tandridge Lane and follow this road for 1.75 miles (3 kilometres), turning right into Crowhurst Lane at the traffic lights by the Brickmaker's Arms. St George's Church stands 1 mile (2 kilometres) down Crowhurst Lane and is almost hidden from view by the Crowhurst Yew in the churchyard.

From Brighton seafront, take the A23 north. Preston Park is on the east side of the road about 2 miles (3 kilometres) from the seafront. These two trees are immediately adjacent to the A23, in the north east corner of the park.

Preston Park Twins

ELM

Wood engraving by
C Dillon McGurk, c1920.

These two fine English elms (*Ulmus minor* var. vulgaris) are the largest remaining elms in Britain and are rare survivors of the 1970s Dutch elm disease epidemic which killed 25 million of these once familiar trees. Thanks to stringent control measures to limit the spread of the disease around Brighton and Hove, there are still 20,000 elms of various species left in the area, the largest population in the country.

Some forms of elm were brought here by Bronze Age farmers, up to 5000 years ago, from south-east Europe where the tree is native. Viable seed is seldom produced in Britain and the tree reproduces vegetatively, usually by suckering from an extensive root system, resulting in genetically identical trees. Thus some suckering hedgerow elms probably consist of genetic material planted during the Bronze Age.

Although all of Brighton and Hove's elms are constantly under threat from Dutch elm disease, these fine specimens are still growing well. They are both just over 20 feet (6 metres) in girth and their survival is a testament to the efforts of those who imposed the control measures. They stand as a living monument to all the English elms which were historically a special part of our landscape.

Queen Elizabeth I Oak

The Queen Elizabeth I Oak, a huge squat hollow tree, is one of the largest trees in Britain and grows on the Cowdray Estate in West Sussex. Cowdray spans some 16,000 acres of land of which 36% is woodland.

As well as the forested areas, Cowdray contains areas of ancient parkland where this veteran sessile oak (*Quercus petraea*) is reputed to have been visited by Queen Elizabeth I, who is said to have been amazed at its size and girth. Verifying this story has proved extremely difficult but, whatever its size at that time, this remarkable tree now has a massive girth of 41 feet (12.5 metres). This makes it one of the largest oaks in the country, rivalled only by the Bowthorpe, Marton and Pontfadog oaks, featured elsewhere in this book. It is in fact the biggest sessile oak in the UK. Its girth in 1947 was 37 feet 11 inches (11.5 metres) and in 1997 was 40 feet 1 inch (12.3 metres). It is therefore still growing despite its advanced years.

However, unlike the other trees, this oak remained relatively unknown until its first recorded measurement in about 1940. [1] Owen Johnson suggests in his book that the growth rate of the known measurements suggests an age of over 1000 years. [1] He qualifies this by suggesting that the widening gap on the south of the tree may have inflated its girth and therefore its calculated age. Despite its hollow centre, the tree continues to thrive close to a footpath across the estate.

Take the A272 from Midhurst towards Petworth. After driving about 1 mile (1.5 kilometres) across the Cowdray estate there is a lake on the left. Park by the lake and take the footpath to the north-west, where the tree can be found in the fields.

The Selborne Yew

The renowned naturalist, clergyman Gilbert White, published his *Natural History and Antiquities of Selborne* in 1789. In this book (which has been continuously reprinted ever since) he recorded the girth of the yew *(Taxus baccata)* in St Mary's churchyard, Selborne, as 23 feet (7 metres) and it became one of the most famous trees in the United Kingdom.

Unfortunately, in 1990 the tree blew over in violent storms, and attempts were made to save it by reducing its crown and re-erecting the remaining tree. Medieval pottery and human remains were found among the roots. As the tree was re-erected a water pipe burst, helping to water the roots. Although the tree survived for a few more years, it eventually succumbed and is now dead.

The stump of the tree still exists and stands as a monument to White, one of the most important of Britain's early naturalists. It is now covered in honeysuckle and ivy, providing an excellent wildlife habitat, and a young silver birch has taken root in the top. The current Vicar of St Mary's, the Reverend John Preston, said recently "With new life sprouting from its heart, the famous yew of Selborne lives on." Elsewhere in the churchyard a cutting from the yew tree is now growing successfully a few metres away to continue the old tree's genetic line.

Selborne is on the B3006, halfway between the A31 turn-off south of Alton, and the A3 turn-off near Greatham, Hampshire. Park at the south end of the village near Gilbert White's famous zig-zag path and walk through the village to the churchyard at the north end.

Wellington's Wellingtonia

Growing in private grounds, the tree can be viewed by appointment. Visiting arrangements can be made by contacting the Administrator, Stratfield Saye House, Hampshire. (Phone: 01256 882882).

The claim to have introduced the Wellingtonia into Britain is split between two individuals – William Lobb and John Mathews. In San Francisco in 1852 Lobb heard of a hunter having found a grove of gigantic trees. He successfully found the grove and, in December 1853, brought seeds and seedlings to England. His discovery was published on 24th December 1853 in the *Gardeners' Chronicle* as the first account of the tree. However, six months earlier, John Mathews had posted a letter dated 10th July 1853 to his father in Scotland, containing Wellingtonia seeds which his father planted. Almost a year later, on 23rd June 1854, his letter was published in the *Gardeners' Chronicle*. Therefore although Mathews' seeds were the first to arrive in Britain, Lobb was credited with having secured the supply of seeds and seedlings, as with monkey puzzle seeds in 1841 (see page 136).

The Wellingtonia was given its name by John Lindley of the Horticultural Society who recognised it as the world's most impressive tree. He thought it right that its name should commemorate the Great Duke of Wellington, who had died the year before. Lindley therefore gave the tree the name *Wellingtonia gigantea*.

One of the first Wellingtonias in the country, this tree was planted 24th April 1857 by the 2nd Duchess of Wellington, in memory of its namesake, at his Stratfield Saye estate, purchased after the Battle of Waterloo.

Cedar of Lebanon at Childrey

Edward Pococke (1604–1691)

The cedar of Lebanon (*Cedrus libani*), the obligatory specimen tree of the Georgian manor house, was probably first brought to Britain as seed by Dr Edward Pococke, a scholar of Arabic at Oxford University, who made several journeys to Syria in 1638/39. This tree is believed to be the oldest cedar of Lebanon in the country.

Pococke was presented with the Rectory at Childrey by Christ Church College, Oxford in 1642 and "according to unbroken tradition" [1] he planted this tree on his rectory lawn in 1646. There is some confusion in the literature between Edward Pococke (1604-1691) and Richard Pococke (1704 - 1765). Richard is credited with "having planted cedars at Highclear (Hampshire)." [2] However, whilst the early literature does not show that Edward planted cedars, it does show that "he planted a plane in the garden of Lady Margaret, Professor of Divinity," [3] and "a fig at Christ Church Oxford, brought from Aleppo and planted in 1648." [4] It is therefore most likely that Edward, who lived at Childrey and had a penchant for tree planting, did plant this tree, making it one of the few to survive the harsh winter of 1740, which destroyed most of the other cedar trees growing in Britain.

Although it has suffered from storms and snow damage in recent years, the tree is still healthy and continues to produce seedlings regularly.

Growing in private grounds, the tree can be viewed by appointment. Visiting arrangements can be made by contacting the Tree Council (Phone: 020 7407 9992).

Via M4, at junction 15 take the A346 through Marlborough to Savernake forest.
The Big Belly oak is by the roadside halfway through the forest.

The Big Belly Oak

In 1830, Strutt referred to Savernake Forest as "one of the most interesting spots in the kingdom to the lovers of wild wood scenery." [1] The earliest mention of the forest dates from 934 AD, when King Athelstan referred to "the crofts alongside the woodland called Safernoc." With the Norman invasion in 1066, Savernake became the Royal property of William the Conqueror and, like the New Forest, the area was maintained as a Royal hunting preserve. [2]

The Forestry Commission now has a long-term lease on the woodland and within the old "Forest of Savernake" there are many ancient trees which are receiving special care.

This 1100 year old oak *(Quercus robur)* of nearly 36 feet (11 metres) in girth is a well-known and much loved local landmark on the ancient trail – now the A346 – between Marlborough and Salisbury, Wiltshire. According to legend, the devil appears to anyone who at midnight dances naked twelve times anticlockwise around the Big Belly Oak. Unfortunately, the current A346 was built very close to the tree and it has consequently suffered the effects of car crashes and compaction to its roots. To stop the tree from falling into the road it has recently been braced, but ultimately surely it is the road that should be moved.

An Edwardian postcard shows more
peaceful times on the A346.

A wood engraving
of the tree from
*The Antiquarian &
Topographical Cabinet*
(1807).

Wyndham's Oak

W yndham's Oak is one of only a few remaining 'hanging' or 'gibbet' trees in England. There are also a few such trees in Scotland, of which the Blairquhan Dool Tree (page 68) is one.

This pendunculate oak (*Quercus robur*) is named after Sir Hugh Wyndham, who was born in 1603 and was appointed a judge in 1659 by Oliver Cromwell. Wyndham was unpopular, cantankerous and impatient with witnesses and in 1660, after the restoration of Charles II to the throne, was deprived of his judgeship. However, he had made enough money to purchase the manor of Silton in Dorset, near where this tree stands. It is said that the judge used to sit under the tree, or even perhaps in it, to contemplate.

The tree itself is reputed to have a bloody history and during the late 17th century is said to have been a gibbet to hang two supporters of the Duke of Monmouth. In 1685, Charles II died and his Catholic brother James II succeeded to the throne. A revolt started in support of Charles II's illegitimate son the Duke of Monmouth (1685), but it was speedily suppressed, and was confined to the southwest of England. James II sent Judge Jeffreys to try the defeated rebels; the resulting 'Bloody Assizes' made 'Hanging Judge Jeffreys' a name remembered throughout history. Jeffreys hanged over 300 peasants while he shouted, swore and laughed at his victims. He left "some places quite depopulated, and nothing to be seen in 'em but forsaken Walls, unlucky Gibbets and Ghostly Carcasses. The Trees were laden almost as thick with Quarters as Leaves" [1].

This grizzly part of our history is commemorated by this beautiful tree, now standing quietly in a rural Dorset parish.

In the second field to the north east of Silton Church, Dorset, on a public footpath.

Martyrs' Tree in Tolpuddle

Under this historic pollard, the largest sycamore (*Acer pseudoplatanus*) in Dorset, the six Tolpuddle Martyrs – a group of farm labourers – met in 1834 to form one of the first trade unions. The landowners and the government were determined to squash the unions and the martyrs were framed on a trumped-up charge of "administering an unlawful oath, using a law applicable to the Navy, not workers' rights." [1] The martyrs were arrested, tried and sentenced to transportation to Australia for seven years in March 1834. After petitions, protest meetings and newspaper campaigns, they were pardoned by the King and returned after spending three years as sheep-farmers in Australia.

The village green with the Martyrs' Tree and memorial shelter were given to the National Trust in 1934 by Sir Ernest Debenham, since when the Trust has managed the property to preserve the original tree and keep it accessible to visitors. An old pollarded tree, this sycamore requires surgery every few years to rejuvenate its growth.

In 1984, to commemorate the 150th anniversary of the martyrs' struggle, the then General Secretary of the TUC, Len Murray, planted another sycamore in Tolpuddle grown from seed from the original tree.

Take the A35 from Bere Regis towards Dorchester. Leave the main road where indicated to Tolpuddle on the left hand side. In Tolpuddle Village, heading still westwards on the road through the centre of the village, the small village green is on the left hand side where the road forks.

Monkey Puzzle at Bicton

From the M5 take junction 30 signposted Exmouth, Sidmouth, Bicton Park. Take the road signposted Sidmouth/Bicton Park and stay on this road until you reach the village of Newton Poppleford. At the mini roundabout take the right hand turn to Budleigh Salterton and Bicton Park. After 2 miles (3 kilometres), Bicton College will be found on the right hand side. The tree is halfway up the avenue on the right hand side.

This monkey puzzle (*Araucaria araucana*) is part of a spectacular avenue growing at Bicton College in Devon, and is the largest example of the species in the UK. It has a girth of 13 feet (4 metres) and is 85 feet (26 metres) tall.

Monkey puzzles were introduced into Britain by Archibald Menzies. While on an expedition which reached the coast of Chile in 1795, Menzies took "from the dessert table of the Governor" [1] seeds which he later planted, bringing seedlings back to Britain.

The monkey puzzle avenue at Bicton was planted in about 1843 using seeds thought to have been collected by William Lobb in Chile in 1841. Lobb is credited with having rediscovered monkey puzzles in Chile and with having brought back significant quantities of seeds for the nursery where he worked – Veitches in Exeter, at that time one of the foremost plant centres in Europe. Lobb is also credited with having introduced the Wellingtonia to Britain some years later (see page 126).

Originally 50 trees were planted, 25 on each side of the main drive to the house, extending for 500 yards (460 metres) in straight unbroken lines with the trees on one side standing precisely opposite those on the other. Of the original 50 trees, 27 remain and new trees have been planted between them to form a new avenue with the same planting distances when all the originals have gone – hopefully, not for many years. All the new trees have been grown from seed produced from the originals.

Meavy Oak

A wood engraving of the Meavy Oak and church (1834).

The Royal Oak at Meavy, or the Meavy Oak as it is also known, is said by tradition to be a tree known to King John and his followers in the hunt. Nearby, a forerunner to the Royal Oak Inn is thought to have been used by King John as a hunting lodge, giving the tree its royal association. The current inn has existed since 1510, although there is evidence of a brew house on the spot from as early as 1102.

This pendunculate oak (*Quercus robur*) stands opposite the lych-gate of St Peter's Church which was built in 1122, and tradition has it that the tree was used as a Gospel Oak whilst the chapel was being built. Under the tree is the village cross, the original of which is thought to have been erected as a preaching cross in the days before the church was built.

In 1826, it was noted that nine people once dined inside the trunk of the tree, on the authority of the hostess of the Royal Oak Inn, and in 1833 the tree was recorded at 50 feet (15 metres) high and 27 feet (8 metres) in circumference.

In 1834 "this venerable tree, though it has suffered from the touch of age, still continues proudly magnificent.... The lower branches still obey the voice of spring, and spread their living canopy over a large area of ground. The topmost boughs, however, are bare, having long ceased to be hung with the massive foliage which they bore in the days of their young lustihood" [1].

One of the more intriguing references suggests that into the early 19th century the tree was during "the village festival, surrounded by poles, a platform was erected above the tree, the top of which was clipped flat like a table and a set of stairs erected.... On top a table and chairs were placed and feasting took place" [2].

In 1970 the villagers became concerned about the tree's health and paid for the best tree surgeons around to help protect it. This work seems to have paid off, as the Meavy Oak is still thriving in 2004.

By the churchyard entrance in the square, Meavy, Devon.

The Darley Oak

The land on which the Darley Oak (*Quercus robur*) grows was in the Dingle family from the 12th century through to the early part of the 20th century. Understood to be about 1000 years old and the largest oak in Cornwall, this 'knarled ancient' is referred to in original family documents as growing on their land in 1030. In 1727, in Harvey's book of the Parish of Linkinhorne on the edge of Bodmin Moor, it was recorded as being 36 feet (11 metres) in circumference with seven steps leading up to its centre. Polsue, in his ancient history of Cornwall, records that the tree was used for "small pleasure parties in the summer season." The *Western Morning News* in 1933 described it as being 38 feet (11.6 metres), indicating that it had been growing steadily in the intervening centuries. However, since then the tree has not increased in size and its girth is still 38 feet (11.6 metres).

One of the beliefs associated with the tree is that "persons afflicted with divers diseases being passed through the tree" will be cured. It is thought that the tree can cure boils and it is also believed that if a person passes through the hollow stem, makes a wish and then encircles the tree along the narrow path, the wish will materialise in due course. No indications are given about the time span implied by "in due course".

> *Take the B3254 Liskeard/Launceston road to the village of Upton Cross, where the tree can be seen in the private garden of Darley Farm.*

Take the A38 south west from Wellington, Somerset. After approximately 3 miles (5 kilometres) turn right at the signpost to Ashbrittle. Follow the signs in the lanes for a further 3 miles (5 kilometres) to the village of Ashbrittle is reached. The church lies in the centre of the village.

The Ashbrittle Yew

Growing on what many believe to be a pre-Christian burial mound, this 3,000-year old tree is England's largest yew (*Taxus baccata*). The tree consists of a central stem surrounded by six diverging stems and together these measure 40 feet (12.2 metres) in girth, just above ground level.

Local legends suggest that the church was built on a Druid circle and that, after nearby battles, Roman soldiers were buried in the mound. Somerset tradition also suggests that yew "branches were placed under the deceased and, being evergreen, were beautifully emblematical of the resurrection of the body, (which is) probably a Christianisation of an earlier pagan belief." [1]

The tree, which grows in the quiet churchyard of St John the Baptist at Ashbrittle, Somerset, was mentioned in Georgian and Victorian diaries, and recently inspired the village to celebrate its ancient history. It was the starting point for Ashbrittle craftspeople to carry out projects with villagers and the local school, celebrating both the tree and the area in which it grows. Visitors can see the results of these initiatives in the church and its churchyard.

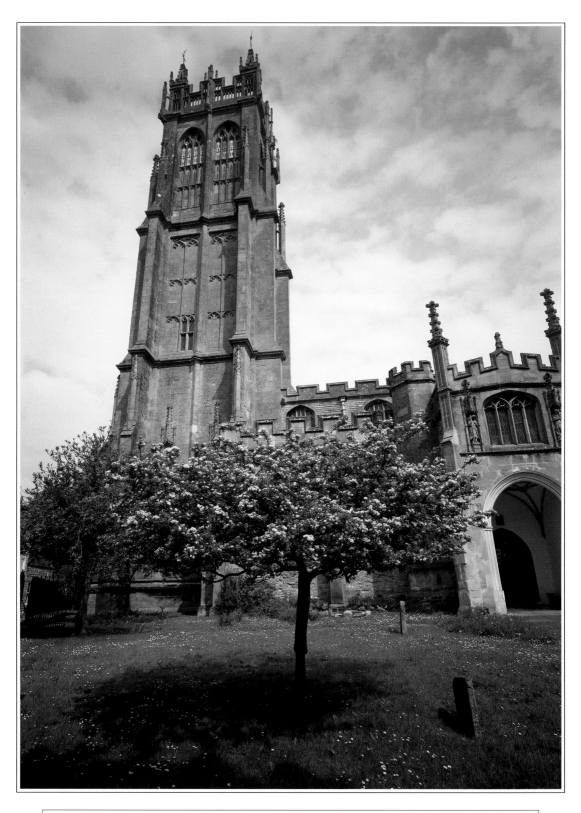

The Glastonbury Thorn can be seen in the grounds of Glastonbury Abbey, Glastonbury, which is open daily throughout the year.

The Glastonbury Thorn

According to Roman legend, after Jesus was laid in the tomb of Joseph of Arimathea, Joseph fled his homeland with a number of followers and made his way to the land of Avalon, an island in the marshes in Somerset. They climbed a hill near Glastonbury, where Joseph is said to have planted his staff to mark his journey's end.

His staff took root and flowered. In AD 63 this miracle was celebrated by the building of the first church in Christendom, dedicated to the Virgin Mary, the forerunner of Glastonbury Abbey. The simple wattle church was built where the abbey's Lady Chapel later stood and grew into the largest and richest abbey in England.

This tree grown from Joseph's staff became the most famous hawthorn in Britain – the Glastonbury Thorn. It is a variety of Common Hawthorn (*Crateagus monogyna* 'Biflora') although the history books have also suggested that it was a variety of Midland Hawthorn (*Crateagus oxycantha* 'Biflora'). It grew on the summit of Wearyall Hill and by Elizabeth I's reign, the offspring from the roots of the original tree, had two main trunks. Unfortunately one of the limbs was removed by a vandal during Elizabeth's reign. Blossoms from the tree were considered such curiosities by people from all over the world that Bristol merchants established a trade in exporting them to foreign lands. The remaining stem was felled by a puritan during Charles I's reign. Many cuttings were taken from it and planted throughout Britain, the most famous being in the grounds of Glastonbury Abbey.

Like the original plant, the Glastonbury Thorn is double flowering and is said to flower in January and again in May. Although this specific tree is not particularly old (probably no more than 90 years old), it is a descendant of the original plant, and hence is a direct link to Joseph and his staff.

A wood engraving from *The Penny Magazine* (1842) which clearly depicts a more mature precursor of the current tree.

Corsham Court Oriental Plane

Corsham Court is one of England's fine stately homes. It was a Royal Manor in the days of the Saxon Kings and the present building is based on an Elizabethan manor. It was built in 1582 by Thomas Smythe, a local man, and was subsequently bought by Paul Methuen in 1745, specifically to provide a storage place for the family art collection.

Methuen employed landscape designer Lancelot 'Capability' Brown to redesign the parklands during the 1760s. Brown laid out avenues and planted the specimen trees including this magnificent oriental plane (*Platanus orientalis*), a species which was brought to England some time before 1562.

In 1907 Elwes wrote of the tree "At Corsham Court, Wilts, the seat of General Lord Methuen, there is an oriental plane with very deeply-cut leaves whose branches spread over a larger area than those of any tree I have seen in England. It is 75 to 80 feet high and 18 feet in girth. One of the branches, which is self-layered in several places, extends no less than 27 paces from the main bole, and the total circumference of the branches is 140 paces" [1].

Elwes' assessment of the tree was correct, for today this magnificent specimen is credited with covering the largest area of any tree in Britain. With an average spread of 210 feet (64 metres), it is as big as a football pitch.

Corsham Court is signposted 4 miles (6.5 kilometres) West of Chippenham from the A4 Bath Road. The grounds are open from late March until September daily except Mondays (but including Bank Holidays) from 2.00 pm until 5.30 pm. From October until late March open weekends from 2.00 pm until 4.30 pm. Admission charges apply.

Westonbirt Lime Tree

The oldest small-leaved lime (*Tilia cordata*) in Britain is a coppiced tree growing in Silk Wood, part of Westonbirt Arboretum. Planting in the arboretum was started by the Holford family in 1829. All the Holford family had a great love of trees and three generations of the family created one of the best tree collections in the world.

In 1956, five years after the death of Lord Morley (Robert Holford's great nephew), Westonbirt passed to the Crown in lieu of death duties and then to the Forestry Commission. After this short period of neglect the Forestry Commission restored the tree collection to its former glory and opened it to the public. Today Westonbirt attracts more than 370,000 visitors annually. The collection has more then 3,700 different plants, represented by some 18,000 numbered individuals and was given National status in 2000.

While working at the Arboretum in the 1970s, John White, Westonbirt's then Curator, became intrigued by an area of small-leaved lime coppice in the woods. He decided to enlist the help of Cambridge academic Oliver Rackham and they undertook a DNA analysis of the huge 52 feet (16 metres) coppice 'stool'. To their amazement they discovered that it was in fact all one tree, estimating its age to be much more than 2,000 years – the oldest lime in Britain. Therefore, although the Holfords brought many amazing trees to Westonbirt, perhaps the most amazing one of all was already growing there naturally.

Westonbirt Arboretum is situated 3 miles (5 kilometres) from Tetbury, Gloucestershire, on the side of the A433 Bath road. The small-leaved lime is located in the area known as Silk Wood. Once in the arboretum, get a free map from the Great Oak Hall or shop and staff will indicate the location of the tree. Admission charges apply.

The Tortworth Chestnut

rowing in a field close to the quiet churchyard in Tortworth, this is probably the most famous and extraordinary sweet chestnut *(Castanea sativa)* in Britain. According to legend it sprang from a nut planted during the reign of King Egbert in 800 AD. Written records of the tree go back to the 12th century and it is supposed to have been a boundary marker to the Tortworth estate "in the time of King Stephen." [1]

Throughout history the tree has often been measured and illustrated. In 1766 Peter Collinson, then Britain's leading dendrologist, described the Tortworth chestnut as "the largest tree in England, being 52 feet around." He went on to say if we pay "regard to an old tradition of the three periods given to the oak and chestnut, viz.

Three hundred years growing.
Three hundred years standing.
Three hundred years decaying.

It countenances my conjecture, that this venerable chestnut is not much less than a thousand years old." [2]

In 1853 the tree was described as "a celebrated tree" [3] and it is one of only two trees named on Ordnance Survey maps of the late 1800s, the other being the Fortingall Yew (see page 22).

In 1788 it seems to have comprised three main stems, but these have since collapsed and deteriorated so that its girth now is only about 36 feet (11 metres). Protective fencing around the tree has allowed it to root freely from its branches and the effect is like walking into a small chestnut wood-land, yet all the growth is from a single tree. This is an example of 'growing down', natural subsidence of the branches leading to layering and longevity.

A West View of the Old Chesnut-Tree at Tortworth in Gloucestershire.

Copper engraving from *The Gentleman's Magazine*, July 1766.

This is probably the earliest rendition of an ancient tree which is still standing, in Britain, although it would appear to bear very little resemblance to the tree today.

In a field adjacent to the churchyard in Tortworth, Gloucestershire, just a few miles east of M5 junction 14.

Croft Castle Oak

This beautiful ancient tree is one of the famous trees growing in the grounds of Croft Castle. Surrounding the castle is a landscape of ancient parkland, embellished with avenues of chestnut and oak. One of these famous avenues is of pollarded sweet chestnuts, known as the 'Spanish Chestnuts', which stretch for half a mile (1 km) to the west of the castle. It has been suggested that this avenue was originally planted from nuts salvaged from the wrecks of the Spanish Armada in 1592, making some of the trees 400 years old.

This giant sessile oak (*Quercus petraea*), quietly nestling in an overgrown hollow in a corner of the estate, was overlooked for a long time by tree recorders. Because the stem is heavily burred and lumpy, it is difficult to be accurate when recording its girth, but it averages just over 42 feet (13 metres), between 4 and 6 feet (1.2 and 1.8 metres) from the ground. In their recent book The Tree Register of the British Isles have recorded its girth at 37 feet (11.3 metres), taking the height above the burrs [1].

Unlike the two other ancient English sessile oaks featured in this book, the Queen Elizabeth's Oak (page 122) and the Marton Oak (page 86), which are entirely hollow, this tree is still largely intact. Deciding which one of these three trees is the largest in England would be difficult, as they are all hard to measure. Indeed, it may be pointless to try, as all are monsters and each in its own way is an extraordinary tree.

About 140 yards (130 metres) to the north of this tree is another famous oak, Sir William's Oak, a large ancient pollard growing near the tennis court. Elsewhere on the estate other ancient pollards can still be found in the depths of the more recent forestry plantations and in pastureland above the Castle.

> *Approach from B4362, turning north at Cock Gate between Bircher and Mortimer's Cross, Herefordshire. This is signposted from the Ludlow–Leominster road (A49) and from A4110 at Mortimer's Cross. The Oak stands in a hollow, 500 yards (460 metres) south west of the Castle. Parking fee £2 for entrance to castle grounds.*

Bewdley Sweet Chestnut

This astounding tree has a current girth of 33 feet 8 inches (10.2 metres) and spreads over no less than a quarter of an acre in the grounds of Kateshill House, Bewdley, Worcestershire. What makes the tree really exceptional is the spread of its branches, which have been allowed to grow unchecked. The longest branch, which stretches down the slope on which the tree grows, has an elbow which touches the ground 44 feet (13.4 metres) from the tree and reaches to its furthest extent 77 feet (23.5 metres) from the tree.

The house was once part of Tickenhall Manor, the home of Prince Arthur, Prince of Wales, son of Henry VII. One version of the tree's history is that it was planted to commemorate Prince Arthur's proxy wedding with Catherine of Aragon (who later married his brother, Henry VIII). Another theory is that the tree was planted in 1567 by Sir Henry Sidney, Lord High Admiral of England, to celebrate the birth of a daughter.

Whilst this sweet chestnut (*Castanea sativa*) has previously lived in relative obscurity, its current owners are now running a bed and breakfast business at Kateshill House, so in future this amazing tree will get the admiration that it deserves.

Growing in private grounds, the tree can be viewed by appointment. Visiting arrangements can be made by contacting the Tree Council (Phone: 020 7407 9992).

The Whitty Pear

The history of The True Service (*Sorbus domestica*) in Britain is an unusual one. For many years the only known tree in the wild was a specimen called 'The Whitty Pear', growing in a remote part of Wyre Forest in Worcestershire. This tree was described in 1678 by Mr. Pitt, who says that "he found it in the preceding year as a rarity growing wild in a forest of Worcester, and identified it with the *Sorbus pyriformis* of L'Obelius, a tree not noticed by any preceding writer as a native of England" [1].

Nash, in 1781, refers to the tree in the Wyre forest as occurring "in the middle of a thick wood belonging to Mr. Baldwyn, which I suppose to be the *Sorbus saliva pyriformis*, mentioned by Mr. Pitt in the Philosophical Transactions for 1678, called by the common people the Quicken pear tree" [1].

Loudon, in 1834, illustrates the tree which he says is "of great age and is now in a state of decay, being 45 feet tall and 1 foot 9 inches in girth" [2]. The Rev. Josiah Lee, rector of the Far Forest, recalled that the old inhabitants of the district, where it was called the 'Whitty Pear tree', used to hang pieces of the bark round their necks as a charm to cure a sore throat. The tree was burnt down in 1862 by a fire kindled by an angry poacher, who wanted revenge on a local tree-loving magistrate.

Various seedlings had been grown from the tree and a replacement grown from its seed was planted in 1916, close to the original spot in the forest, and is still growing well.

In 1983 a botanist, Marc Hampton, discovered a tree he did not recognise growing on a Glamorganshire cliff. There were several wind-trimmed, small and partially prostrate trees which were difficult to identify, but careful study revealed them to be *Sorbus domestica*. Initially, it was thought that they were introduced specimens, but ring counts from dead branches showed that the trees were extremely slow growing and indicated that they may be as much as 400 years old.

Given this evidence, and the cliff location of the trees, it seems likely that the True Service is in fact a rare native species and that both the Whitty Pear and the Glamorgan trees could be descended from the same 'edge-of-range colonising stock' that has now declined to a few remnant populations.

Call at the Callow Hill Visitor Centre in the Wyre Forest, where a map can be collected which gives details of the Forest Trails and the location of the Whitty Pear. The Centre can be found approximately 2 miles (3 kilometres) west of Bewdley, Worcestershire on the A456.

Royal Oak at Boscobel

This 1930s postcard shows the Royal Oak in its prime, with Boscobel House in the distance.

This Royal Oak growing in the grounds of Boscobel House is a direct descendant of the celebrated tree in which Charles II hid after the Battle of Worcester in 1651. In an account dictated to the diarist Samuel Pepys in 1680, King Charles described the tree as "a great oak that had been lopt some three or four years before, and being grown out again, (was) very bushy and thick." [1]

The story of the future King and the oak spread and attracted many 17th century visitors who took away pieces of the tree as souvenirs. Indeed, Blount said that "this tree was divided into more parts by Royalists than perhaps any oak of the same size ever was, each man thinking himself happy if he could produce a tobacco stopper, box etc made of the wood." [2]

A protective wall was built around the original tree in 1680, and within the wall a young English oak (*Quercus robur*) began to grow from the Royal Oak's acorns. The original tree was removed by about 1740 but the young tree continued growing. In 1817 the wall was replaced by the present circular iron railing. The replacement Royal Oak is therefore a direct link to the original tree that protected the fleeing King and has been celebrated for 260 years.

The Royal Oak can be found signposted off the A5 near Weston Park, north east of Telford, Shropshire. Follow signs from A5 for 1 mile (1.6 kilometres) to Boscobel House. The tree is in the grounds of the house. Open daily 11am – 6pm (March – November). Admission charges apply.

Powis Castle is located approximately 1 mile (1.6 kilometres) south of Welshpool, Powys. The castle is in the care of the National Trust and is well signposted off the A483. The deer park forms part of the privately owned Powis Estate and restricted access is available on recognised routes. 'The Powis Oak' stands next to the exit drive around 220 yards (200 metres) from the castle.

The Mighty Oaks of Powis Castle

The 'Powis Oak' (main picture)
and 'Gwen Morgan's Oak' (above).

The extensive deer park of Powis Castle, on the Welsh marches, is renowned for its many fine specimen trees. Oak in particular thrives on the fertile soil and the estate is home to some exceptional specimens of great size and antiquity.

A sessile oak (*Quercus petraea*) in the prime of life occupies a commanding position on a low knoll looking towards the red sandstone ramparts of the castle. Known as the 'Powis Oak', it encapsulates the robust and rugged beauty of a species deeply enshrined in the cultural history of the UK. The trunk measures 25 feet 8 inches (7.8 metres) in girth and the storm-battered crown reaches a height of 66 feet (20 metres). Typical of maturing oaks, it is starting to assume a stag-headed appearance as the outer extremities of the upper branches gradually die back. Huge, hawser-like roots anchor the tree to its rocky outcrop.

Other notable oaks in the grounds include 'Lady Powis' Oak', measuring 25 feet 5 inches (7.8 metres) in girth, and 'Gwen Morgan's Oak'. The latter has recently been re-pollarded to prevent the hollow and decayed trunk shattering under the increasing weight of the limbs.

The Buttington Yew

The yew (*Taxus baccata*) with the oldest known planting date in Britain stands within the churchyard of All Saints Church, Buttington. It was reputedly planted in 846 to mark the Battle of Buttington, at which the English under King Alfred the Great, and the Welsh, under King Merfyn of Powys, besieged and defeated the Viking invaders of Prince Hastein. In 1838, when the school was built in the south west corner of the churchyard, 400 skulls and an array of other bones were unearthed, presumably those of unfortunate victims of the conflict.

The yew, a male, is a fine specimen with a full, healthy canopy. The single trunk measures 29 feet 6 inches (9 metres) in girth at 5 feet (1.5 metres) from ground level, and is certainly of a size consistent with its supposed vintage. The trunk is hollow, a common feature of most ancient yews, and is filled with decades of accumulated litter and humus.

In the churchyard of All Saints Church, Buttington, Powys, at the junction of the A458 Welshpool/Shrewsbury Road and the B4388.

163

The Pontfadog Oak

Wales's largest sessile oak *(Quercus petraea)*, at 42 feet 5 inches (12.9 metres) in girth, has a long history. Tradition says that in 1165 the Welsh Army gathered under the shade of this enormous tree before fighting the English invaders under Henry II at the battle of Crogen a mile to the east.

In 1850 the tree's owner apparently discovered two gold chisels which had been hidden in the trunk. Although they were said to be on view locally in 1880, the fate of the chisels is now unknown. The current owner recalls that, as a teenager in 1963, she heard a loud noise and thought the chimney had fallen over. In fact, a large limb of the oak had fallen on the farmhouse. The tree later deteriorated and the International Hermeneutic Society, whose members frequently visited the oak, sponsored the fitting of a supporting band to the crown, which is still in place.

The tree was measured in 1971 by the renowned botanist Roy Lancaster and subsequently appeared in the 1972 *Guinness Book of Records* as the largest oak in Britain.

In 1999, two saplings grown from acorns collected by Tanya Austin of Llangennech were presented to the National Botanical Garden of Wales. Pontfadog Primary School, Wrexham, has also adopted the oak as a logo.

Growing in private grounds, the tree can be viewed by appointment. Visiting arrangements can be made by contacting the Tree Council (Phone: 020 7407 9992).

The Gresford Yew

The churchyard of All Saints Parish Church, Gresford, Wrexham, Denbighshire.

A wood engraving of the Gresford Yew from
Arboretum et Fruticetum Britannicum by J.C. Loudon (1854).

The ancient yew (*Taxus baccata*) in Gresford Churchyard, Wrexham, is undoubtedly a fine and imposing specimen. Its huge trunk and shapely, elegant form has attracted the attention of chroniclers over the last few centuries. Writing in 1836, Bowman observed that "It is a male tree, in good condition, and is reputed to be the finest of its specie in Wales"[1]. In 1842, Selby observed, "The Gresford Yew stands pre-eminent for its beauty of form and magnificent appearance; it grows in the south east corner of Gresford Churchyard, near Wrexham, Denbighshire, and has a circumference a little below the divarification of the branches of 29 feet, and at the very base, 22 feet"[2].

The yew, enclosed in iron railings, still supports a full and spreading canopy and casts a dark shade over the weather-worn gravestones at its foot. It is thought that it may be as much as 1600 years old.

One theory as to the origin of the tree suggests that it was planted around 350AD by the widow of a Roman officer, who had been stationed at nearby Chester. A carved stone was placed over his grave, and the yew was planted as a symbol of immortality[3].

The churchyard is home to many fine old yew trees, although none yet match the size and grandeur of the veteran.

The Three Sisters

'The Three Sisters' is the affectionate name given to three sweet chestnuts (*Castanea sativa*) which grew shoulder to shoulder in the fertile parkland near Ruthin. Thought to have been planted around 1660, the trio had already become a well-known landmark by the end of the 18th century. The great traveller and observer Thomas Pennant noted in 1781 in his 'Tour of Wales' that they were "fine chestnut trees, one of which is near 24 feet in circumference" [1]. It is thought that the trees may have been planted by Lord Salisbury who lived at nearby Bachymbyd Fawr, one for each of his daughters.

Alas, one of the sisters was felled by the beginning of the 19th century and the sun-bleached, skeletal remains of another lie uprooted on the ground, a victim of the elements. Only a squat, hollowed out shell not much more than 12 feet (4 metres) high remains of the sole surviving sister. Despite the loss of a large section of the trunk through decay and old age, it nevertheless boasts an exceptionally large girth of 42 feet and 6 inches (13 metres). The fire-blackened interior of the shell testifies to a troubled past. However, vigorous new growth from low side branches continues to keep this old survivor alive.

In the private garden of a property known as 'The Three Sisters', on the A525 Ruthin to Denbigh Road, approximately 1 mile (1.6 kilometres) south of Pentre-Llanrhaeadr, Denbighshire.

The Pulpit Yew

The tranquil hamlet of Nantglyn, nestling in the rolling hills of Denbighshire, North Wales, is home to a most remarkable yew tree (*Taxus baccata*). The hollowed trunk of this ancient specimen has been turned into an al fresco pulpit, literally reinforcing the connection between this species and places of worship. Crude steps fashioned from the local slate lead into the hollow interior of the tree through a large, natural gash in the trunk, culminating in a raised seat and podium. Standing within the heart of the tree the elevated position provides a panoramic view of the churchyard and the ancient gravestones scattered around the base of the trunk. Legend has it that sermons were preached from the improvised pulpit, including one by John Wesley (1703 - 1791), founder of the Methodist Church (see the Wesley Beeches, page 72). One observer noted in the 1850s, "There has been an aperture on one side of this tree, which is now built up with lime and stone, and forms a sort of armchair, where an active party may climb and sit and view the beauties of the pretty little vale" [1].

Despite the intrusive building works, the yew continues to flourish and its full, luxuriant canopy dwarfs the modest, slate-clad church. The trunk measures 27 feet 3 inches (8.3 metres) in girth.

In the churchyard of St James Parish Church, Nantglyn, Denbighshire, on the B5435 approximately 5 miles (8 kilometres) south west of Denbigh.

St. Digain's Church, Llangernyw, is on the A548, about half way between Abergele and Llanrwst, and stands next to the Stag Hotel.

The Llangernyw Yew

Estimated to be up to 4,000 years old, this huge yew is the oldest tree in Wales. As with many ancient yews, its trunk has split into several parts, joined at ground level by only a thin strip of bark. The tree's current girth has been measured at 36 feet (11 metres).

The Llangernyw yew (*Taxus baccata*) stands in the small churchyard of St Digain's, in the village of Llangernyw, north Wales. Despite its huge size and age, the tree somehow remained unnoticed by previous natural historians. Unexpectedly, this remarkable yew tree was 'discovered' in 1995, by Jon Stokes and his colleague Kevin Hand, during a training day for Tree Wardens in the former county of Clwyd.

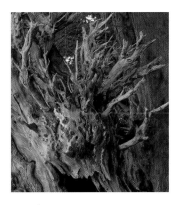

A detail of the inside of the tree.

At that time there was a large oil tank in the centre of the hollow stem. The Tree Council arranged for the tank to be removed in order to protect the tree, as part of the 1995 National Tree Week celebrations. A memorial stone to celebrate this "Green Monument" was erected in the churchyard and unveiled on 25th November 1995.

Since its discovery the Llangernyw Yew has brought many visitors to this quiet Welsh village.

Pennant Melangell Yews

Four ancient yew trees (*Taxus baccata*) brood silently over the mysterious and atmospheric graveyard at Pennant Melangell, a remote hamlet dominated by the surrounding hills. The trees, two male and two female, are thought to be as much as 2000 years in age and predate the Christian church. The trees support full, healthy canopies, although the gnarled trunks and limbs are much decayed and hollow.

The site takes its name from Melangell, a saint from Ireland who founded the first small church in 607. Legend has it that one day a prince named Brochwell was hunting in a place called Pennant, when his hounds gave chase to a hare. On pursuing it, he came across a virgin praying, with the hare taking refuge under the folds of her clothing. The prince urged the hounds on but they fled howling, and when he raised his hunting horn it stuck fast to his lips. The virgin informed the prince that she was seeking refuge and sought to live in the area. The prince was so humbled by her godliness that he granted the valley to her and there she founded a religious community. Animals, particularly hares, were said to seek sanctuary and safety in the valley and became known as 'Melangell's lambs'. Her church became a place of pilgrimage and healing – a tradition which continues to this day.

The church site is steeped in history and was a Bronze Age site long before the advent of the Christian Church. The ancient yews stand in silent witness over this special place.

The Shrine Church of Saint Melangell, Pennant Melangell. The village lies 2 miles (3.2 kilometres) along a narrow winding road west of the village of Llangynog, Powys, on the B4391.

Dafydd ap Gwilym's Yew

The Cistercian Abbey at Strata Florida, Cardiganshire, founded in 1184 by Rhys ap Gruffyd, is known to have been surrounded by 39 great yew trees up to the middle of the 16th century. However, by the end of the 19th century, only two of this original number survived [1].

The larger is a female (*Taxus baccata*) which stands within a low stone wall next to the chapel. The huge trunk, which measures 23 feet (7 metres) in girth, is very decayed and the canopy has become rather scrappy and tattered. Surgery has been carried out to prolong the life of the tree, and it is showing promising signs of recovery.

This yew has become a well-known specimen due to its association with the renowned Welsh medieval poet Dafydd ap Gwilym (c. 1320 – c. 1380), who is reputed to be buried beneath it. A small carved stone set within the hollowed trunk commemorates his final resting place. The abbey was strongly supported by the Welsh princes and was a focus for literary activity and influence.

A smaller male yew stands approximately 200 feet (60 metres) north east of Dafydd's yew. While the trunk is much smaller in girth, it is a surviving fragment of a much larger tree and is probably of similar age to its near neighbour. No exact records exist as to the age of these two survivors, although it is thought that they predate the abbey and may have been associated with an earlier Welsh settlement. This could make them up to 1500 years old [1].

> Within the grounds of Strata Florida Abbey, approximately 1 mile (1.6 kilometres) east of the village of Pontryhdfendigaid, Cardiganshire, on the B4343. The abbey is in the care of CADW (Welsh Historic Monuments) and is open throughout the year.

A small carved stone set within the hollowed trunk commemorating Dafydd ap Gwilym's final resting place.

The Bleeding Yew of Nevern

Eight old yews (*Taxus baccata*) line the short path which leads from the church gate to the door of St Brynach's Church, Nevern. Their twisted trunks and dark canopies intertwine to create a dark and sombre tunnel. No records exist of their planting, but they are thought to be around 600 years old.

The famous 'bleeding yew' is the second tree on the right hand side on entering the church gate. It enjoys this rather grisly title due to a red, blood–like exudate which oozes from a wound on the trunk about 6 feet (2 metres) from ground level.

This slowly trickles down the bole, congealing and forming a black crust as it dries. This strange phenomenon has given rise to various tales and legends. One of these alleges that a monk was hanged from the tree. While declaring his innocence he is said to have stated "If you hang me guiltless as I am, these trees will bleed for me" [1]. Another suggests that it is the result of a condemned man's hand being cut off.

This strange exudate is likely to have a more mundane natural explanation. Rainwater and the by–products of decay trapped in the hollow trunk have become stained by the red heartwood and found an exit route through the old pruning wound. Subsequent colonisation by various yeasts has resulted in a thick, blood–like fluid.

A detail of the 'bleeding yew'.

Also within the churchyard is a fine row of 26 Irish yews (*Taxus baccata* 'fastigiata'), standing to attention (see also Original Irish Yew, page 74). These were planted in 1928 in memory of the members of the parish who perished in the Great War.

In St Brynach's Church, Nevern, Pembrokeshire, on the B4582, approximately 8 miles (13 kilometres) east of Fishguard.

Aberglasney Yew Tunnel

row of yew trees (*Taxus baccata*) has been transformed into a most remarkable feature at Aberglasney, Carmarthenshire. The branches of a short row of about six individual trees have been bent over to the ground on one side to form a natural arch. As the branches have taken root and the trees have matured, the evergreen foliage has created a dark tunnel down which it is possible to walk. Regular clipping has maintained the shape of the tunnel and enhanced the mystery of the interior. With time, the trunks and branches of the trees have become fused and knotted to form a living sculpture, and a feature probably unique in the UK. In its heyday, the yew tunnel must have formed an intriguing novelty for visitors and guests to the house.

The trees were recently discovered to be younger than originally thought. Ageing using dendrochronology (see the Lochwood Oaks, page 70) puts them at around 250 years, the period when the house was in the ownership of the Dyer family [1].

Aberglasney House and its gardens have had a long and chequered past. Changes in ownership in the 1950s witnessed a period of dramatic decline and the once immaculate gardens became lost under a jungle of weeds. It was only during restoration work in the 1990s that the yew tunnel was rediscovered. A programme of management is now in place to restore the overgrown yews gradually to their original form.

Llangathen, Carmarthenshire. The gardens are signposted off the A40, approximately 10 miles (16 kilometres) east of Carmarthen. The gardens are owned by the Aberglasney Restoration Trust and are open to the public throughout the year. Admission charges apply.

The tree stands within a hedgerow approximately 220 yards (200 metres) from
Talley Abbey (in the care of CADW), signposted off the B4302 approximately
6 miles (10 kilometres) north of Llandeilo, Carmarthenshire. From the abbey car
park, walk through the adjacent churchyard and out of the far gate. Follow the
footpath along the side of an old hedge for approximately 220 yards (200 metres)
and the ash stands on the left, immediately through a field gate. It can be readily
viewed from the public footpath which passes by the tree.

The Talley Abbey Ash

This leviathan is one of the largest ash trees (*Fraxinus excelsior*) known in the UK. Standing within an overgrown hedgerow close to the picturesque ruins of Talley Abbey, its massive trunk presents a unique challenge to the tree measurer. The various swellings and contortions of its twin stems provide vastly differing statistics depending at what point a tape can be threaded around the trunk. This varies from 25 feet (7.8 metres) at six feet (two metres) from ground level to an impressive 36 feet (11.0 metres) when measured at 3 feet (one metre) [1]. Nothing is known of the age or origin of this specimen, although it is clearly older than most trees of the species, which is not known for its longevity. Its formidable frame is draped in a dense cloak of ivy and the remarkable bulk of the trunk is not readily obvious, surrounded as it is by hedgerow vegetation.

Indigenous to the UK, ash is a common feature in hedgerows. Its timber is remarkably tough and strong, and is traditionally used for tool handles and sports equipment, such as hockey sticks and oars.

As well as its utilitarian value, ash is deeply enshrined in the mythology of northern Europe, where it is known as the legendary Yggdrasill, or World Tree. It was thought to symbolise the universal link between the dead, mankind and the gods, and conceptually marked the centre of the universe. It was seen as a 'guardian' tree and was often planted near homes and sacred sites. Legend has it that Odin, the Norse god, hung from Yggdrasill for nine days and nights in order to learn its hidden knowledge and wisdom.

The nearby ruins of Talley Abbey

Ley's Whitebeam

This Ley's whitebeam *(Sorbus leyana)* is one of only 16 representative of this species growing wild anywhere in the world, making it Britain's rarest tree. The species is also classed internationally as Critically Endangered and it is protected under the 1981 Wildlife and Countryside Act.

All 16 Ley's whitebeams grow in the Taff Valley in Wales amongst the rocky limestone crags. The species was discovered here by the 19th century botanist, the Reverend Augustine Ley (1842-1911), after whom it is named.

There are 20 Sorbus species in Britain of which the whitebeam *(Sorbus aria)*, the rowan *(Sorbus aucuparia)* and the wild service tree *(Sorbus torminalis)* are the most common. Of the other 17 species, 15 are endemic which means that they are found naturally only in Britain. Many of these species are among Britain's rarest trees, and their distribution is very limited (see the Arran whitebeams, page 50).

This rare Great British Tree grows near the Forest Enterprise's Garwnant Visitor Centre. Fortunately the tree is in a public area and so can be enjoyed by all who wish to see it, but visitors should remember that it is our rarest tree, and are asked to treat it with care and respect.

Take the A470 from either Brecon (heading south) or Merthyr Tydfil (heading north). Take the turning to Garwnant Visitor Centre, which is signposted from the A470. Follow the minor road over the bridge to the Visitor Centre. The tree is outside the Rangers office with the plaque in front of it.

The Bettws Newydd Yew

The tranquil churchyard of Bettws Newydd is home to three ancient male yew (*Taxus baccata*) trees. Each is a fine specimen, but it is the largest of the three next to the church footpath which is the most intriguing. Not only is it of great sculptural beauty but it also demonstrates one of the unique survival mechanisms of the species.

Ancient yew trees are invariably hollow, the redundant heartwood broken down by the relentless process of decay over many years. However, this natural phenomenon need not sound the death knell for the tree, as there are many hollowed out yews in good health throughout the UK. Occasionally, yews will generate new internal roots which travel down the hollowed interior of the original trunk. These take root in the rich mulch of accumulated decayed material to provide a new source of life. Thus the tree effectively recycles itself. In theory, it could continue to do so in perpetuity.

This novel method of regeneration is apparent on the venerable specimen at Bettws Newydd. A robust, healthy new trunk has developed within the bleached and skeletal framework of the original tree. This 'tree within a tree' was already well-established as far back as 1876 and now measures 7 feet 6 inches (2.3 metres) in girth. A representation of the tree dating back to 1890 shows remarkably little change in over a century. In such situations, it has been found that increase in girth of the original trunk effectively ceases, as the new 'tree' takes over [1]. The original shell of this specimen, although much decayed, is one of the few known yew trees in the UK to exceed 30 feet (9 metres) in girth.

The graveyard of the Parish Church of Bettws Newydd, located within the village of Bettws Newydd, off the B4598 approximately 4 miles (6.5 kilometres) north of Usk, Monmouthshire.

References

The Kilravock Castle Layering Beech (p.16)
1 Miles, A. *Silva*. Ebury Press 1999.

The Fortingall Yew (p.22)
1 *Philosophical Transcations of the Royal Society*. Vol 59, Dec 1769. p.23.
2 Neil, Dr: *Edinburgh Philosophical Journal*, 1833.
3 Loudon J C: *Arboretum et Fruticetum Britannicum or The Trees and Shrubs of Britain*. London, 1854. p.2079.

The Parent Larch (p.26)
1 *Account of the larch plantation on the estates of Atholl and Dunkeld. Executed by the late John, Duke of Atholl*. Perth, 1832.
2 Mitchell, A. *Alan Mitchell's Trees of Britain*. Harper Collins, 1996. p.73.

The Scone Douglas Fir (p.32)
1 Elwes H. and Henry A: *The Trees of Great Britain & Ireland*. Edinburgh, 1906-13 p.83.
2 Mitchell: p.73.

The Mightiest Conifer in Europe (p.36)
1 Evelyn J: *Silva: or a Discourse of Forest Trees, and the Propagation of Timber in his Majesty's Dominions*. Royal Society, 15 October 1662.
2 *Transactions of the Scottish Arboricultural Society*. Volume ix: p.174.
3 Elwes and Henry: p.730.

Robert the Bruce's Yew (p.38)
1 Danielewski J: *Loch Lomond in Old Picture Postcards*. 1987.

Inchmahome Veterans (p.40)
1 Hunter T: *Woods, Forests and Estates of Perthshire*. 1883. p.311.

The Clachan Oak (p.42)
1 Highland and Agricultural Society of Scotland: *Old and Remarkable Trees in Scotland*. 1867. p.177.

Stephenson's Yew (p.54)
1 *'To Minnie', A Childs Garden of Verses*, 1885.
2 *'The Manse', in Memories and Portraits*, 1887.

Newbattle Abbey Sycamore (p.56)
1 Mitchell: p.184.

The Kailzie Larch (p.64)
1 *Principle Excursions of the Innerleithen Alpine Club during the Years 1889-94.*

The Wesley Beeches (p.72)
1 Conservation Volunteers Northern Ireland: *Remarkable Trees of Northern Ireland*. 1999.

Great Yews at Crom (p.76)
1 Elwes and Henry: p.123.
2 Loudon: p.2081.
3 Conservation Volunteers Northern Ireland: *Remarkable Trees of Northern Ireland*.

The Borrowdale Yew (p.78)
1 *North Lonsdale Magazine and Furness Miscellany*, April 1886.

The Marton Oak (p.86)
1 Lyson D & Lyson S: *Magna Britannia Cheshire*. Cadell & Davies, London, 1810.

The Major Oak (p.88)
1 Rooke, H: Descriptions and Sketches of Some *Remarkable Oaks, in the Park at Welbeck, in the County of Nottingham, a Seat of His Grace the Duke of Portland*. J Nichols, London, 1790.
2 Wilks J H. *Trees of Britain in history and legend*. Muller, 1972, p.170.

Newton's Apple Tree (p.92)
1 de Voltaire F M A: *An essay upon the Civil Wars of France extracted by curious manuscripts*. London, 1727.
2 Turnor, E: *Collections for the history of the town and soak of Grantham*. 1806.
3 Keesing R G: *The history of Newtion's apple. Contemporary Physics*, Volume 39 1998, pp.377 – 391.

Bowthorpe Oak at Bourne (p.94)
1 Mitchell: p.313.

Ely's London Plane (p.96)
1 Elwes and Henry: p.621.

The First Dawn Redwood (p.98)
1 Professor Merrill: *Arnoldia*. Vol 8 No 1, 1948.
2 *Journal of the Royal Horticultural Society* Vol LXXIII part 7, 1948.
3 Cambridge University Botanic Garden Website.

Hethel Old Thorn (p.102)
1 Elwes and Henry: p.1738.
2 Grigor, J: *Eastern Arboretum*. P. 282. 1841.
3 Elwes and Henry: p.1738.
4 Johnson, O. (ed): *Champion Trees of Britain and Ireland*. 2003. p.49.

Ankerwycke Yew at Runnymede (p.110)
1 Strutt J G: *Sylva Britannica; or, Portraits of Forest Trees, distinguished for their Antiquity, Magnitude, or Beauty.* London 1830.
2 Lowe J: *The Yew Trees of Great Britain and Ireland.* London 1897.

Charlton House Mulberry (p.114)
1 Loudon: p.1345.

Sidney Oak at Penshurst (p.116)
1 *Country Gentleman's Magazine* May 1794 No 5 Vol LXIV Pt. 1.

The Crowhurst Yew (p.118)
1 Evelyn: p.199.
2 Chetan A and Brueton D: *The Sacred Yew* Penguin 1994.
3 Brailey: *History of Surrey.* Vol IV p.132.
4 Lowe: p.201.

Queen Elizabeth I Oak (p.122)
1 Johnson O: *The Sussex Tree Book.* Pomegranate Press 1998.

Cedar of Lebanon at Childrey (p.128)
1 Cornish C J: *Lebanon's Cedars and their seed.* Country Life May 2nd 1903.
2 Loudon: p.2426.
3 Ward J: Dr Pococke's Trees: *The Gardeners' Chronicle, Gardening Illustrated.* Dec 28th 1957.
4 Loudon: p.1367.

The Big Belly Oak (p.130)
1 Strutt: p.28.
2 Walwin, P. C: *Savernake Forest.* 1976.

Wyndham's Oak (p.132)
1 *The Western Martyrology.* (A Whig Pamphlet) 1705.

Martyrs' Tree in Tolpuddle (p.134)
1 Tolpuddle Martyrs Museum.

Monkey Puzzle at Bicton (p.136)
1 Elwes and Henry: p.47.

Meavy Oak (p.138)
1 Hearder, G. & J. *The South Devon Monthly Museum.* Plymouth, July 1st, 1834. VOL. IV. No. 19. pp.1-2.
2 Harris, E and Harris, J: *Oak – A British History.* p.191. Windgather Press 2003.

The Ashbrittle Yew (p.142)
1 Hartzell H: *The Yew Tree: A thousand whispers.* Oregon 1991. p.116.

Corsham Court Oriental Plane (p.146)
1 Elwes and Henry: p.622.

The Tortworth Chestnut (p.150)
1 Evelyn: p.203.
2 *The Gentleman's Magazine.* July 1766. Sylvanus Urban, Gent.
3 Loudon: p.1999.

Croft Castle Oak (p.152)
1 Johnson: p.91.

The Whitty Pear (p.156)
1 Elwes and Henry: p.148.
2 Loudon: p.922.

Royal Oak at Boscobel (p.158)
1 Thomas G C: *An account of His Majesty's escape from Worcester. Dictated to Mr Pepys by the King Himself.* London, 1894.
2 Blount T: *Boscobel; or The History of His Sacred Majesties Most Miraculous Preservation after the Battle of Worcester, 3 Sept. 1651. Introduc'd by an exact Relation of that Battle.*

The Gresford Yew (p.166)
1 Wilks: p.105.
2 Selby: *British and Foreign Trees.* 1842. p.377.
3 Baxter, T: *The Eternal Yew.* 1992. p.156.

The Three Sisters (p.168)
1 Pennant, T: *Tour of Wales.* 1781.

The Pulpit Yew (p.170)
1 Griffiths, E: *Nantglyn.* 1984.

The Llangernyw Yew (p.172)
1 Rev J Humphreys: *Western Mail,* 5th July 1935.

Dafydd ap Gwilym's Yew (p.176)
1 Bevan-Jones, R: *The Ancient Yew.* 2002. pp.62-75.

The Bleeding Yew of Nevern (p.178)
1 Wilks: p.88.

Aberglasney Yew Tunnel (p.180)
1 David, P: *Aberglasney: A Garden Lost in Time.* 1999.

The Talley Abbey Ash (p.182)
1 Johnson: p.57.

The Bettws Newydd Yew (p.186)
1 Bevan-Jones: p.25.

Index

The Tree Council

The Tree Council was set up in 1974 as an umbrella body for organisations to work together for the trees that are such a vital part of the urban and rural landscape. The aim was to keep up the momentum of National Tree Planting Year, with its campaign slogan of 'Plant a Tree in '73' — itself a response to the devastation being caused by Dutch elm disease.

A registered charity, the Tree Council is dedicated to inspiring, initiating and enabling effective action for trees. It works in partnership with its members, volunteers and supporters to make trees matter to everyone. It also organises initiatives to plant more trees — of the right kind and in the right place — and campaigns for better care for all trees, of all ages. Its Tree Warden volunteer force is particularly important in spearheading many Tree Council activities.

For further information visit www.treecouncil.org.uk or contact The Tree Council, 71 Newcomen Street, London SE1 1YT, email: trees.matter@treecouncil.org.uk.

Acknowledgements

The Tree Council and the authors would like to record their thanks to the owners, managers and supporters of the various trees for their willing assistance in providing and confirming information, without which this book could not have been produced. We are also indebted to the many Tree Wardens and members of the public who brought some of the lesser known trees to our attention.

The Tree Council would like to express thanks to those involved in the 'Great British Trees' and 'Heritage Trees of Scotland' projects, the research for which has made a major contribution to this volume. In particular, thanks are extended to Mike Steele of The Tree Council, Caroline Davis of the Ancient Tree Forum, Derek Patch of The Tree Advice Trust, James Ogilvie, Charlton Clark and James McDougall of the Forestry Commission Scotland and Jeanette Hall of Scottish Natural Heritage.

We are indebted to the Forestry Commission Library at Alice Holt Lodge; The Garden magazine; to Harvard University; to the Royal Horticultural Society Library; and to the TUC Library.

We are also grateful to David Alderman of the Tree Register of the British Isles who provided valuable information on many of the trees.

Finally, we would like to pay special tribute to Peter Branchflower whose individual contribution in time, care and effort helped to ensure the completion of the book.

Photographs ©
Archie Miles: Cover and pp. 2, 8, 11, 12, 13, 14, 16, 22, 26, 28, 33, 40, 41, 45, 46, 49, 53, 67, 68, 71, 72, 74, 75, 76, 77 (main), 78, 79, 80, 83, 85, 86, 90, 91, 92, 98, 102, 105, 108, 113, 114, 125, 126, 129, 130, 136, 137, 138, 141, 142, 149, 150, 153, 154, 156, 157, 159, 160, 161, 163, 164, 165, 172, 173, 175, 182, 183, 184, 185, 187.
Edward Parker: pp. 18, 19, 20, 25, 31, 34 (both), 36, 38, 43, 50 (both), 51, 55, 56, 58, 61, 63, 64, 84, 89, 95, 96, 99, 101, 107, 110, 115, 116, 118, 120, 122, 133, 135, 144, 147, 166, 169, 170, 177 (both), 178, 179, 180.
Jon Stokes Collection: pp. 23, 24, 27, 32, 60, 66, 93, 100, 104, 111, 117, 119, 127, 131, 132.
Archie Miles Collection: pp. 88, 106, 109, 121, 124, 145, 151, 158, 167.
Courtesy Felix Dennis Collection: pp. 57, 103.
Tim Winter Postcard Collection: pp. 29, 39, 42, 62.
NHPA Limited: p.112.
Ulster Museum: p.77 (inset).
Exeter Central Library (Local Studies Collection): p.139.
Courtesy Mr and Mrs J. Linsley: pp. 54, 58 (inset).
Courtesy Revd. and Mrs J. Hutton: p.73.
Courtesy Levens Hall: p.82.
Courtesy The owners of the Marton Oak: p.87.
Courtesy The Diocese of Ely: p.97.
Courtesy St. Mary The Virgin Church, Childrey: p.128.
Courtesy The TUC (designed by Peter Gill and Associates): p.134.